SRI SHIRDI SAI B
The Universal Master

This is an up-to-date, comprehensive and research-based book on the divine life, miracles and teachings of Sri Shirdi Sai Baba who was a unique Incarnation of God descended on earth during 1838-1918. The author has highlighted in an analytical manner the significance of Sri Shirdi Sai Baba as the Universal Master whose message transcends all traditional religions and cults and unites and elevates all people spiritually and morally.

Prof. Satya Pal Ruhela is Professor of Education, Jamia Millia Islamia (Central University), New Delhi. He is an ardent Sai devotee and has contributed a number of books on spirituality, sociology and education.

By the same author

1. *What Researchers Say on Sri Shirdi Sai Baba* (1994)
2. *The Sai Trinity* (1994)
3. *The Educational Theory of Sri Sathya Sai Baba* (1994)
4. *Sai Baba & His Message* (1994)
5. *Sri Shirdi Sai Baba Avatar* (1992)
6. *My Life with Sri Shirdi Sai Baba: Thrilling Memoirs of Shivamma Thayee, 104 Years Old Lady, the Direct Devotee of Sri Shirdi Sai Baba* (1995)
7. *Sri Sathya Sai Baba & The Future of Mankind* (1992)
8. *Sri Sathya Sai Baba: Lehre, Leben and Werk* (In German, 1992)
9. *The Emerging Concept of Education in Human Values* (1996)
10. *The Sai Baba Movement* (1991)
11. *Sai Baba on Human Values & Education* (1996)
12. *In Search of Sai Divine—A Comprehensive Research Review of Writings & Researches on Sri Sathya Sai Avatar* (1996)
13. *Sai Baba & the Press* (1996)
14. *Sai System of Education and World Crisis* (1995)
15. *Immortal Quotations of Bhagavan Sri Sathya Sai Baba: A Spiritual Ready Reckenor* (1996)

Sri Shirdi Sai Baba
The Universal Master

DR. S. P. RUHELA

A Sterling Paperback

STERLING PAPERBACKS
An imprint of
Sterling Publishers (P) Ltd.
L-10, Green Park Extension, New Delhi-110016
Ph.: 6191784/5, 6191023 Fax: 91-11-6190028
E-mail: sterlin.gpvb@axcess.net.in

Sri Shirdi Sai Baba: The Universal Master
©1994, Dr. S.P. Ruhela
ISBN 81 207 1624 8
Reprint 1995, 1996, 1998

All rights are reserved. No part of this publication may be reproduced, stored in a retrieval system or transmitted, in any form or by any means, mechanical, photocopying, recording or otherwise, without prior written permission of the publisher.

Published by Sterling Publishers Pvt. Ltd., New Delhi-110016.
Lasertypeset by Rasleen Art Printers Pvt. Ltd., New Delhi-110008
Printed at Print India, New Delhi.
Cover Printed at Roopak Printers, Delhi.
Cover design by Jayant Kumar

*THIS HUMBLE FLOWER
OF
MY LOVE, DEVOTION AND DEDICATION
IS
MOST HUMBLY AND REVERENTIALLY DEDICATED
TO
THE LOTUS FEET
OF
SRI SHIRDI SAI BABA*

Preface

"Om Sai, Sri Sai, Jaya, Jaya, Sai."

Sri Shirdi Sai Baba, the universally worshipped *Avatar* (Incarnation of God), who during His advent (1838-1918) in India, taught the basic of morality and spirituality to mankind and promoted a unique kind of unity and integration amoung the Hindus, Muslims and members of all other communities through His simple yet powerful teachings of *atmic* unity, love, compassion, *rinanubandha* (bondage of give and take), *saburi* (patience), *shraddha* (faith), *samarpan* (surrender), *sambhava* (equanimity), *vairagya* (detatchment), *dakshina* (donation) and *karma punarjanma* (action and rebirth).

His external appearance of a simple, illiterate rural Faqir who lived in an old, dilapidated and isolated mosque at Shirdi, which He named 'Dwarka Mai', putting on tattered clothes like a Muslim faqir, begging alms twice or thrice from five fixed houses and performing all sorts of thrilling miracles to cure, help and bless His countless devotees and visitors drawn from all communities, was in fact a grand veil of *Maya* (Illusion) projected by Him to hide His real stature of a *Poornavatar* (Full or Integral Incarnation of God).

Sri Shirdi Sai Baba was the re-incarnation of Lord Dattatreya, Lord Shiva, and Saint Kabir - the great iconoclast saint and poet of the Bhakti period of medieval India. He was *Sarvadevtaswaroopam* (all Gods rolled into One), inaugurator of spiritual renaissance in the Kali age, and the first of the Sai Trinity. His powerful impact as a word redeemer is being felt in ever-growing proportions throughout the world.

It was my good fortune to have come under the umbrella of the divine grace of Sri Shirdi Sai Baba and that of his contemporary re-incarnation Sri Sathya Sai Baba. I first came under Sri Sathya Sai Baba's grace in 1973 and through His discourses and writings, I learnt about Sri Shirdi Sai Baba. Ever since my first visit to Shirdi in 1974, I developed a deep love for and faith in Sri Shirdi Sai Baba, and wish emerged in my heart to write on Him.

It was in July 1992 that Baba, by His divine grace, brought me in contact with Sri H.D. Lakshmana Swamiji of Bangalore during a train journey on my way to Sri Sathya Sai Baba's *ashram* at Puttaparthi. Swamiji became a source of my inspiration by kindling my wish and taking me to Her Holiness Shivamma Thayee, 102 years old lady and the sole/surviving direct devotee of Baba. Her revelations and blessings not only made my task easier but also enabled me to publish her thrilling memoirs. Later Swamiji took me to Shirdi to seek Sri Shirdi Sai Baba's sublime blessings at His *Samadhi Mandir* on the auspicious day of 13 August, 1992. I was also fortunate to receive the blessings of His Holiness Shivnesh Swamiji who lives at Sai Baba's famous *Chavadi* and *Gurusthan*. The Executive Officer and the Public Relations Officer of Sri Shirdi Sai Sanathan also blessed and encouraged me.

Even though there have been spells of trials and tribulations, lack of funds and innumerable other problems, yet with *saburi* (patience) and *shraddha* (faith), the bountiful grace of Sri Shirdi Sai Baba steered my boat and it has been possible to bring out this book of my cherished desires. In all humility, I lay this humble effort at the Baba's Lotus Feet in a spirit of total surrender and complete egolessness.

I am grateful from the core of my heart to Sri H.D.Lakshmana Swamiji, Her Holiness Shivamma Thayeeji and Sri N. Ramu, an ardent Sai devotee—all from Bangalore, for their unique blessings and motivation.

I am much greatful to His Holiness Shivnesh Swamiji and the Executive Officer and the Public Relations Officer of Sri Shirdi Sai Sansthan, all of whom blessed and encouraged me for the success of this project.

I have been greatly helped by Professor P.S. Verma, my colleague in the university, Professor Adhya Prashad Tripathi, Head, Department of Hindi, Sri Sathya Sai Institute of Higher Learning, Prasanthi Nilayam, and Sri M.V. Shastri, Manager of Quick Photocomposers, New Delhi — all of whom are ardent Sai devotees. I am really privileged to have their valuable friendship and love.

My uncle (Late) Sri Narendra Singh Verma and my wife, Smt. Sushila Devi Ruhela, also have been of great help to me in this work and I am very much thankful to them.

Preface ix

A number of Sai devotees from India and abraod encouraged and helped me in various ways in this work. I am especially thankful to Smt. Santosh Shanker, Chief of the Editorial Department of Vikas Publishing House, New Delhi; Sri Aziz Qureshi, Former Minister of Education, Madhya Pradesh; Col. H.P. Singh of New Delhi; Mr. William E. Armitage of Montreal (Canada), Mr. John Hopfgrater of Wien (Austria); Charles McDonald of Omaha (USA); Sri M.R. Kundra of London; and innumerable other friends and well-wishers from Germany, Mauritius, South Africa and Australia who are all ardent devotees of Sri Shirdi Sai Baba.

Careful thanks are also due to all writers and publishers of books, and articles on Sri Shirdi Sai Baba from whom I have immensely benefited.

I offer my heartfelt gratitude to Sri S.K. Ghai, Managing Director, Sterling Publishers, who went out of his way to encourage me to write this book, when most publishers showed least interest. I also convey my deep appreciation to Colonel B.L. Chuni (VSM), who painstakingly edited this book.

Invoking Baba's holy Name and seeking His blessings, I have pleasure in placing this humble flower of Baba's grace in the hands of Sai devotees and spiritual seekers. May Baba shower His choicest love and blessings on each one of them.

Satya Pal Ruhela

Sai Kripa
126, Sector 37,
Faridabad-121003

Contents

	Preface	vii
1.	Introduction	1
2.	Spiritual Heredity	9
3.	Origin	19
4.	Childhood	28
5.	Sojournings	33
6.	Charismatic Personality	44
7.	Devotees	62
8.	Contemporary Saints	81
9.	Thrilling Miracles	90
10.	Unique Teachings	101
11.	The Universal Master	115
12.	Popularity	128
13.	*Appendices*	
	I. Pilgrimage to Shirdi	137
	II. Baba's Worship : 108 Names of Sai Baba	140
	III. A Select Bibliography	144

I am Parvardigar (God). I live at Shirdi and everywhere. My age is lakhs of years. My business is to give blessings. All things are Mine. I give everything to everyone.

—Sri Shirdi Sai Baba

1
Introduction

SRI Sai Baba of Shirdi was born on 27 September, 1838, in a forest near Pathri village in Aurangabad district of Maharashtra, formerly the State of Nizam of Hyderabad. His parents were high-caste Brahmins of the Bharadwaja *gotra*. His father's name was Ganga Bavadia. His parents and even grandparents had worshipped their family deity, Hanuman of Kumhar *bavadi* (water tank), on the outskirts of Pathri village. It is possible that because they lived near the *bavadi*, they were known as Bavadia (one who owns or lives near a *bavadi*). Baba's parents' house (No. 4-438-61) situated in Vaishnav Gali has been bought by the local people, who formed "Shri Sai Smarak Mandir Samiti" and erected a shed where local Sai devotees now perform *arti* (worship) of Sai Baba every Thursday.

Sai Baba's father, Ganga Bavadia, was a poor boatman of Pathri. His mother was Devagiriamma. The religious parents not only worshipped Hanuman but also Lord Shiva and Shakti. They did not have a child for many years after marriage. Suddenly, one night Lord Shiva and Shakti came to their house when Devagiriamma was alone, her husband having gone to the riverside to save his boat from the rainy and stormy night. The divinity blessed Devagiriamma with three children and assured that Lord Shiva Himself would be born as her third child. As a result of this divine blessing, one son and one daughter were born to Devagiriamma. While the third child was yet to be born, her husband developed *vairagya* (detachment) and decided to forsake his family and go away to the forest to worship God.

Devagiriamma also decided to follow her husband. She sent her two children to her mother's house and accompanied him to the forest. The couple had hardly gone a few miles when birth pangs set in. She implored her husband to wait for a while, but he kept going his way. Devagiriamma delivered the child all alone in the forest under a banyan tree, placed the newborn, covering it with leaves, on the ground and leaving it there, hastened after her husband. Sri Sai Baba so told His devotees about His mother :

My mother was greatly rejoicing that she had got a son (i.e., Me). I was, for My part, wondering at her conduct. When did she beget Me? Was I begotten at all? Have I not been already in existence? Why is she rejoicing as such?

Sai Baba's mother rejoiced on His birth even though she was abandoning Him forever in the forest. It was because she knew that the third child, now born was, according to the blessings received earlier, Lord Shiva himself, so what need had she to worry when the child was divine?

Hardly had a few minutes passed when an elderly Muslim *faqir* named Patil, returning with his wife from His in-law's place in a *tonga* (horse cart), reached the very spot where the newborn child was lying enveloped in leaves. The *faqir's* wife *faqiri* alighted from the tonga to ease herself. She was surprised to hear the soft cries of a newborn babe. Excited by such a revelation she called her husband to the spot and showed him the baby. As they were childless, they at once thought that *Allah* (God) had sent that baby for them; they took the child with them to their house in Manwat village and brought it up as their own son.

The *faqir* died after four years. After her husband's death *Faqiri* was at the tether's end, as the child, christened 'Babu', was always up to strange and abnormal acts offensive to her religion. He would go to the Hindu shrines and recite the *Quran*, or instal a stone Shivalinga in a mosque and worship it or play marbles and win a Saligram from the moneylender's son, or sing songs in praise of Allah in Hindu temples and say "Rama is God, Shiva is Allah" and so on. Puzzled at such behaviour and with scores of daily complaints from Hindus and Muslims against Babu, Faqiri eventually decided to carry Babu to Sailu and entrust Him to the charge of a pious and spiritually elevated Brahmin, Guru Venkusha, who was running an *ashram* for the orphaned, abandoned and poor boys of all communities. Actually, Venkusha's real name was Gopala Rao Deshmukh. In one of his earlier births, he had been the famous Hindu

Introduction

Guru Ramananda of the medieval saint Kabir while Shirdi Sai Baba Himself had been his disciple Kabir at the time.

Babu stayed at Guru Venkusha's *ashram* for about 12 years, i.e., from 1842 to 1854. He was much loved by His Guru because of His staunch devotion. Sai Baba told one of His devotees, Radha Bhai Deshmukh, about His Guru Venkusha in these moving words:

> I had a Guru. He was a great saint and most merciful. I served him long, very long; still he would not blow any *mantra* into my ears. I had a keen desire, never to leave him, but to stay, serve him at all costs and receive some instructions from him.
>
> I resorted to my Guru for 12 years. He brought me up. There was no dearth of food and clothing. He was full of love, nay he was the love incarnate. How can I describe him? When I looked at him he seemed as if he was in deep meditation and then both of us were filled with bliss. Night and day, I gazed at him with no thought of hunger and thirst. Without him, I felt restless. I had no other object to meditate on, nor any other thing than my Guru to attend to.
>
> He never neglected me, but protected me at all times. I lived with him and was sometimes away from him, still I never felt the want or absence of his love...

Because of Guru Venkusha's great love for Babu, other boys of the *ashram* grew jealous of Him. Once, when Babu had been sent by Venkusha to fetch *bilva* leaves from the forest for worship, a group of boys overpowered Him; they beat Him up and one boy even hit Him on His forehead with a brick which started bleeding profusely. The other boys fled away from the scene. He took the brick with Him and came to Guru Venkusha who was deeply grieved to see Babu in this miserable condition. He tore a *dhoti* (loin cloth) and bandaged the wound on His forehead. He shed tears at the brick which had hit Babu's head. Thereafter, Venkusha advised Babu to leave his *ashram* with warm blessings, unlimited divine powers and directions. He gave Him the brick and a piece of cloth and directed Him to go towards the Godavari river.

Thus, one evening in 1854, Babu left Guru Venkusha's *ashram* all alone taking the brick with Him, and within a few days reached Shirdi on foot. An old woman of Shirdi, the mother of one Nana Chopdar, who saw this 16 years old ascetic, left behind this description:

> This young lad, fair, smart and very handsome, was first seen under the *neem* (margosa) tree, seated in an *asana* (yogic posture). The people of the village were wonderstruck to see such a young lad

practising hard penance, not minding heat and cold. By day he associated with none, by night he was afraid of none... outwardly he looked very young but by his actions he was really a great soul. He was the embodiment of dispassion and was an enigma to all...

He stayed at Shirdi barely for two months and one day suddenly left the place. He wandered from place to place for a few years without disclosing His identity to anyone. Most of His followers and devotees till today do not know any details of His activities during those unknown years. The Baba, however, once told His close devotees:

When I was a youngster, in search of bread and butter, I went to Badaum. There I got an embroidery work. I worked hard, sparing no pains! The employer was very much pleased with me. Three other boys worked before me. The first got Rs. 50/-, the second Rs. 100/-, and the third Rs. 150/- while I was given twice the whole of this amount. Seeing my cleverness, the employer presented me a full dress, a turban for the head and a *shawl* for the body, etc. I kept this dress intact without using it. I thought that what a man might give does not last long and is imperfect but what my *Sircar* (Lord) gives, lasts to the end of time.

In a forest near the twin villages Sindhon-Bindhon, 24 kms south of Aurangabad, a Muslim, Chand Patil, resident of Dhoop Kheda village, met the young *faqir* (Sai Baba) who did the fascinating miracle of calling Patil's lost mare 'Bijli' and materialising live charcoals by thrusting a pair of tongs into the earth. Chand Patil invited the young *faqir* (Sai Baba was then dressed like a Muslim *faqir*) to his village Dhoop Kheda. At Dhoop Kheda, He performed a number of thrilling miracles.

After some days, He accompanied Patil's party to Shirdi in bullock carts, where the marriage of Patil's nephew was to take place.

That very morning, Mlahaspati, the priest of Khandoba temple in Shirdi, welcomed the return of the *faqir* after four years and spontaneously addressed Him by uttering the words "Ya, Sai" (Come, Sai), and since that memorable day He came to be known as Sai Baba of Shirdi. He made Shirdi His permanent abode and physically never went out beyond a radius of five miles. He achieved the *Nirvana* (the cessation of individual existence) on Tuesday, the 15th of October, 1918 on the Dussehra festival day. He thus lived for 80 years, from 1838 to 1918, as a mortal.

It was during His permanent stay at Shirdi from 1858 to 1918 that He performed all His thrilling *leelas* (divine sport), miracles, spiritual transformation and granted *mukti* (liberation) to innumerable

Introduction

creatures — human beings, animals, insects, etc. all drawn to Him as if by magic. He lived like a Muslim *faqir* in an old deserted mosque which He named as "Dwarka Mai Masjid". He begged for alms twice or thrice a day from only five chosen houses, and shared His food with His devotees as well as those animals and birds which lived in His ambience. His external appearance, as a grand veil of *maya* (illusion) was that of a *faqir* — simple, illiterate, traditional, moody, emphathetic — at times fiery and abusive — at others, full of humane concern and compassion. He enacted all this simple yet charming divine drama for six decades, all this to hide His real identity as the God incarnate.

The deception did not work because the villagers of Shirdi and His devotees from all over Maharashtra and South India soon succeeded in finding out His reality as an *avatar* of a very high order. Rarely did He declare publicly that He himself was God; most of the time He behaved as if He was a servant of God : *"Allah malik hai"* (God alone is the Lord and Master). But He once demonstrated that He was the incarnation of Lord Dattatreya — the three-headed son of Sage Atri and his wife Anasuya, a combined incarnation of the Trinity : Brahma, Vishnu and Shiva. He also revealed that He had been Saint Kabir of the 14th-15th centuries in one of His previous births. To many of His devotees, He demonstrated that He was in fact, *Sarvadevtaswaroopam* (all gods and goddesses rolled into one). He demonstrated through His breathtaking miracles how He was present in all the forms of gods and goddesses and saints of all faiths. He gave these solemn assurances to everyone for all times to come, in the following words:

> Whosoever puts his feet on the soil of Shirdi, his sufferings would come to naught.
>
> I shall be active and vigorous, perpetually and forever, even after leaving this earthly body.
>
> My tomb shall bless and answer to the needs of My devotees.
>
> I am living forever, to help and guide all those who come to Me, who surrender and seek refuge in Me.

Like Paramahansa Yogananda's Guru's Guru Mahavatar Babaji, Sai Baba is still in this world in His spirit form, occasionally assuming His physical body and make-up as the Sai Baba of Shirdi robed in white, to guide, help and encourage His devotees of all faiths, to do good deeds in their lives. This fact has, time and again, been testified by the articulation of innumerable Sai devotees in India and abroad; their testimonies and miracles have been printed in several journals, books and souvenirs during the last seventy-six years. The spiritual saga of Sai Baba of Shirdi is today fast spreading to all the corners of the world. Shirdi Sai Baba temples have been established in most of the Indian townships and across the oceans in metropolises like London (UK), Los Angeles (USA), Loredo (USA), Canberra (Australia), Durban (South Africa), Lagos (Nigeria), etc. Today, among His large number of devotees are Germans, Austrians, Africans, New Zealanders, who are all enamoured with His unlimited wealth of spirituality and simple personality.

It is indeed a most thrilling and challenging mystery for all spiritual seekers, intellectuals and Sai devotees of all faiths and countries to unravel, understand and appreciate how living and working within the traditional rural social context of Shirdi of the late 18th and early 19th centuries, the humble Sai Baba of *Dwarka Mai Masjid* emerged as the most powerful and influential spiritual Messiah, universal for the entire humanity, who inaugurated an era of spiritual awakening in the world.

We may recall that Shirdi Sai Baba's sojourn on the earth from 1838 to 1918 was during the most difficult and thorny period of the history of human civilisation. Industrial revolution had proliferated exploitation by the colonial powers of the underdeveloped countries throughout the world. The First World War was fought and there was unmitigating misery and violence spreading far and wide. In India, the British rulers, the Rajas, Nawabs, Jagirdars and their puppets and instruments of exploitation were sucking the blood of their subjects. The first battle of India's Independence in 1857 was fought by patriots like Rani Lakshmi Bai of Jhansi, Nana Phadnavis, Bahadur Shah Zafar of Delhi, etc., but the Indians had been defeated in this attempt. The Indian National Congress had taken birth and the Indian patriots had again started their struggle to achieve *Swaraj* (Independence). The dominant features of the contemporary Indian society were ritualism, communal tensions among the Hindus and Muslims, casteism, untouchability, racial segregation, poverty and an overall spectre of gloom.

It is really a wonderful story as to how, without the backing of any powerful religious or political organisation or the support of any patrons, or any specific religious idiosyncrasy or a cult of fanatic zealots and, in the absence of any paraphernalia or great fanfare of guruhood and publicity, Sri Sai Baba of Shirdi, living in the most humble, simple and traditional rural background, single-handedly sowed the seeds of communal amity and harmony. All this was achieved by the basic principles of *atmic* unity, oneness of soul, spiritualisation and attainment of peace and moral dignity by respecting man, regardless of his race, nation or creed

Introduction

in the strifeful society. What He taught through His parables and stories, as also through His brief observations and teachings to His devotees, was the most refined quintessential spiritual religious traditions of all the faiths of mankind presented in a very simple, direct and penetrating words which enlivened every heart.

Who was this Sai Baba of Shirdi in reality? Some say that He was an *avadhoota*, some an *auliya*, some a con man; while some opine Him to be a great and unique saint of the era.

Sri Mehar Baba, who Himself was an important *avatar* and a disciple of Shirdi Sai Baba's most blessed disciple, Sri Upasani Maharaj, said this about Sri Sai Baba:

> You will never be able to uderstand thoroughly how great Sai Baba was! He was the personification of perfection. If you know Him as I know Him you will call Him the Master of creation.

Sri Sathya Sai Baba of Puttaparthi (Andhra Pradesh), whose declaration that He is the incarnation of Sri Shirdi Sai Baba, staunchly believed by millions of His devotees in over 100 countries of the world, revealed this about Sri Shirdi Sai Baba:

> Shirdi Sai was a *Brahma-Jnani*. He was the embodiment of Universal Consciousness - *Jnaneswaroopa*. He was also the *Sadguru*, teaching His devotees the reality, and guiding them along the path of Truth.

> He was a *Poornavatar* (full or integral incarnation) and possessed all the attributes of a *Poornavatar*. He had all the attributes of divine *Shakti* (power) but held them in check and did not reveal them fully. He was like a learned musician who exhibited His musical skill occasionally; He was like a gifted poet who gave voice to His verse only rarely; He was like a skilled sculptor who revealed His artistry only sometimes.

> ...*siddhis* (miracles) and *leelas* (sports) were merely outpourings of (His) love for His devotees. They were not meant to attract but only to safeguard and protect. He did not use them like visiting-cards. He used His *Shakti* only to save His ardent devotees from distress and trouble, from sorrow and pain. His advent was for revealing the essence of true divinity.

To describe such a great divine personality or Prophet is not only a gigantic task but at the same time thrilling and fortunate. It is on record that when Sri Shirdi Sai Baba's ardent devotee, Anna Saheb Dabolkar, sought Baba's permission to write the first book on His divine life and *leelas*, Baba blessed him with these words to Shama, who had pleaded for Hemadpant's request :

> Let him make a collection of stories and experiences, keep notes and memos; I will help him. He is only an outward instrument. I Myself would write My life and satisfy the wishes of My devotees. He should get rid of his ego, place it at My feet. He who acts thus in life, him I help most.
>
> ...Hearing My stories and teachings will create faith in devotees' hearts and they will easily get self-realization and bliss; let there be no insistence on establishing one's own view, no attempt to refute others, opinions, no discussion of pros and cons of any subject.
>
> ...If My *leelas* are written, the *avidhya* (nescience) will vanish and if they are attentively and devotedly listened to, the consciousness of the worldly existence will abate giving place to strong waves of devotion and love and if one dives deep into My *leelas*, he would get precious jewels of knowledge.

I earnestly believe that these words of blessings, guidance and assurance of Sri Shirdi Sai Baba were not for Hemadpant alone who was the author of *Shri Sai Sat Charita*, the first biography of Baba, but also for all the future writers of biographies and books on Him, His devotees, worshippers and all those who would be coming under the umbrella of His grace for all times to come. This great assurance of Sri Shirdi Sai Baba has, in fact, been the motivation for the author to write this book on Him.

> *I embroiled myself in Karma and got this body. Brahman is my father and Maya is my mother. I am formless and in everything. I fill all space and am omnipresent. I am in water, in dry places, in crowds and solitary wilderness. I am in the fire and in ether.*
>
> —Sri Shirdi Sai Baba

2

Spiritual Heredity

SRI Shirdi Sai Baba was not an ordinary saint. He was God descended in human form in 1838. He had revealed that His age was "lakhs of years". He was Himself God, having taken innumerable births previously and had lived in many generations with a number of people who were His contemporaries in Shirdi.

There are four distinct and widely prevalent beliefs about the sprititual heredity of Shirdi Sai Baba:

1. He is considered to be the pure and full incarnation of Lord Shiva.

2. He is considered to be the third incarnation of Lord Dattatreya — the Trinity of Brahma the Creator, Vishnu the Sustainer and Shiva the Destroyer. The first two notable incarnations of Dattatreya were Sri Sripada Srivallabh and Sri Narsimha Saraswati, of the 14th and 15th centuries.

3. He is considered to be in the Nath tradition of great *yogis* which was started by Shiva, Guru Machinderanath and Guru Gorakhnath.

4. He is considered to be the incarnation of Kabir, the great iconoclastic saint of medieval India who laid stress on spirituality without ritualism and communal harmony among all people.

As Incarnation of Lord Shiva

Sri Sathya Sai Baba of Puttaparthi (Andhra Pradesh), who claims himself to be the combined contemporary incarnation of Lord Shiva and *Shakti* (the consort of Shiva) and also the incarnation of Shirdi Sai Baba, narrated the following story publicly in 1968:

> Thousands of years ago, the great sage Bharadwaja, wishing to master all the Vedas, was advised by Indra (the ruler of Gods) to perform a *yagya* (Vedic ritual). Eager to have Shakti preside over it and receive Her blessings, Bharadwaja left for Kailash (a sacred peak in the Himalayas), the abode of Shiva and Shakti, to convey the invitation. Finding them entranced in the cosmic dance, Bharadwaja waited for eight days — apparently ignored by them, and obviously failing to comprehend the welcoming smile cast on him by *Shakti*.
>
> Unhappy and disappointed, Bharadwaja decided to return home, fell in a stroke and his left side was paralyzed as a result of cold and fatigue. Shiva then approached and cured him completely by sprinkling on him water from the *Kamandalu* (vessel). Consoled by Shiva, Bharadwaja was granted boons by both Shiva and Shakti, who were also pleased to attend the *yagya*. Shiva promised the *Rishi* (sage) that they would both take human form and be born thrice in the Bharadwaja *gotra* (religious lineage) — Shiva alone at Shirdi as Sai Baba; Shiva and Shakti together at Puttaparthi as Sathya Sai Baba; and then Shakti alone as Prema Sai... (Rishi Bharadwaja had received this boon about 5600 years ago).

As Incarnation of Lord Dattatreya

In his *Shri Guru Charita,* Acharya E. Bharadwaja recalls a saint Sri Gulavani Maharaja, a direct disciple of Sri Vasudevananda Saraswati, telling him, "He (Shirdi Sai Baba) is the *avatar of Lord Dattatreya.* He manifests Himself to His worthy devotees even today in His physical form and guides them."

The story of Lord Dattatreya is that Anasuya, wife of the great sage *Atri,* became famous for her devotion to her husband *(pativratya).* Such was her spiritual power that even the hard and uneven earth turned soft and smooth for her as she walked over it. Even the scorching sun and blazing fire turned cool in regard to her. The god of wind did not dare to blow except as a pleasant breeze for her sake. The gods presiding over nature's forces were afraid that they would lose their dignity if they defied her greatness and so sought refuge from Lord Vishnu, the sustainer of all existence.

Spiritual Heredity

Once Sage Narada, who freely moves in the three worlds, visited the abodes of Brahma, Vishnu and Shiva and proclaimed the spiritual eminence of Anasuya which was a result of her intense and unrivalled devotion to her husband and of her unfaltering vow of hospitality to visitors. Hearing this, the consorts of the divine Trinity, i.e., Saraswati, Lakshmi and Parvati, felt jealous of her and wept. When their husbands tried to console them, they insisted that they should find an occasion to curse Anasuya Devi, or trap her in moral dilemma and see that her greatness did not exceed theirs. So the three Gods went to the hermitage of Sage *Atri*, disguised as three random guests *(atithis)*. Anasuya welcomed the guests with due respect and seated them. As per her vow of dutifulness, she said, "Holy Sirs, you have sanctified our hermitage by your holy visit. I heartily welcome you. Please say what I can do for you. The master of the hermitage, Sage Atri, has gone to the forest to perform his austerities *(tapas)*." The guests told her that they were all very hungry and could not wait till her husband returned. They wanted to eat immediately. She went in and after making proper arrangements invited them to lunch. Then the guests said, "Holy one! Unless you take off your clothes and serve us food in your nakedness, we shall not eat but go away hungry!" On hearing their words, she smiled to herself and reflected thus: "I am totally purified by the long association with Sage Atri. What harm can the god of lust ever do to me? So I need fear nothing. If I do not comply with their precondition, they would go away cursing me for failure in my duty and my promise to feed them. As they have sought food from my hands, I look upon them as my own children and not as strangers or grown-up men."

Having decided thus, she said to them, "Sirs, I shall do as you wish, come and have your lunch!" Then as she unrobed herself, by virtue of her superior spiritual power, the divine guests were at once transformed into infants. At the sight of them, holy and motherly love swelled up in her heart so intensely that her bosom experienced lactation. She happily suckled them and the three infants were immensely satisfied. Brahma, Vishnu and Shiva, as though exhausted with their tasks of creation, sustenance and destruction had all enjoyed perfect bliss in her lap.

Then Anasuya realised that they were the Holy Trinity and was very happy. She put them in a cradle and rocked it, singing a lullaby recounting the whole incident. Sage Atri, who was on his way home, heard the song from a distance and knew what had transpired. On reaching the hermitage, he glorified the Trinity thus: "Oh, Thou Supreme Spirit! You are the ultimate cause for creation, preservation and destruction.

You are the witness of the whole universe, the omnipresent, all-pervading essence of all existence. You are Lord Vishnu. You are indeed the reality. But by Your divine sport, You manifested as the Holy Trinity for Your own play. Though the universe is a projection of nescience of Your Real Essence, it is not distinct from You. Only when perceived through the illusory sense of 'I and mine', it looks distinct from You."

As he sang thus, even while the three infant forms were in front of him, they also appeared before him in their original forms and wanted him to seek a boon from them. He then looked meaningfully at his wife and said, "My dear, these holy ones cannot be reached even by the mind. They appeared here only by the power of your devotion. Tell them of your heart's wish." She replied, "My Lord, you were created by Brahma for the promotion of the phenomenon of creation. Therefore, I shall be pleased if you pray to the one Lord that has appeared as this Trinity to live as our son." Sage Atri did so. So the One Spirit, manifest as the trio said, "Oh wise sage, I offer Myself to you henceforth as your adopted Son. Hence I am Datta". (In Sanskrit, Datta means the adopted son.)

In order to denote that Datta was his son, he came to be known as Dattatreya. He is indeed the Supreme Lord Himself, the goal of the Vedas. He is of the nature of Reality-Awareness-Bliss. He is the Master of Yoga and wisdom, the wish-fulfiller of His devotees and wandering all over the creation ever ready to bless them at their mere thought of Him.

The Supreme Spirit, henceforth known as Dattatreya, is indeed unbound by phenomenal existence. Yet, in deference to a curse laid on Him once by Sage Durvasa, He ever abides on earth, assuming different human forms. This He does out of compassion for the creatures on earth and for the gods.... Thus Dattatreya is the eternal *Avatar* of God's spirit and self-dedication to the salvation of all creatures. He manifests Himself perennially as the perfect Saint of all religions of the world.

Sri Shirdi Sai Baba is believed to be the third prominent incarnation of Dattatreya. It is said that His contemporary saint, Swami Samarth of Akkalkot (1800-1878), was also an incarnation of Dattatreya. The essence of Sai-Datta philosophy is the "oneness of the individual soul with the universal soul".

Iconographically, Dattatreya is shown surrounded by animals including dogs that also figure in the symbolism of Sai Baba. It may be recalled that dogs were favourites of Shirdi Sai Baba. At Shirdi even now it is considered to be an act of religious piety on the part of Sai devotees to offer milk to the dogs near the famous Dwarka Mai Masjid of Shirdi Sai Baba. In many pictures of Shirdi Sai Baba, a dog is shown seated near Him. Many devotees had experienced that Baba often went to their houses, when invited for lunch, in the form of a dog; many a time the hosts discarded or hit the dog out of their ignorance not realising that Baba was present in all creatures including those dogs.

As a Great Saint, Nath or Pir in the Nathpanthi Tradition of Saivite Ascetics

In the sacred and most authentic book, *Shri Sai Sat Charita* or *The Wonderful Life and Teachings of Sri Sai Baba* (English translation), the English translator, Nagesh Vasudev Gunaji, has written that Sri Shirdi Sai Baba was Chief of the Nath-Panchayatan at that time:

> It is said that a few centuries ago, there was a *Daspanchayatan* (group of five saints) consisting of Samarth Ramdas, Jayaramaswami, Ranganathaswami, Keshavaswami and Anandamurthi. Similarly, it is said that there was *Nath-Panchayatan* in those days, consisting of Madhavnath Sri Sadguru Sainath, Dunddiraj Palusi, Gajanan Maharaj of Shegaum, and Gopaldas (Narsing Maharaj) of Nasik and they all worked together by inner control or force. One Mr. Suman Sunser has also written about this in Sai Leela wherein he says that Sai Nath (Baba) had great respect in this *Panchyatan* and was referred to as Trilokinath and Kohinoor by Madhavnath.

According to Professor Charles S. J. White, Associate Professor of Philosophy and Religion at the American University, Washington D.C., "Gorakhnath's order is peculiar and significant in relation to the Sai Baba movement for several reasons. There is evidence that the *Nathpanthis* have some connection with Islamic asceticism...a principal focus of the community and religious life in a *Nathpanthi* house is the hearth or *dhuni* wherein a fire is kept perpetually burning."

White adds, "Sai Baba was a celibate, remaining in one place, performing miracles, admonishing his disciples and keeping a fire perpetually burning in a *dhuni*. Therefore, it would not be unreasonable to assume that he was following customs already sanctified in the *Nathpanthi* tradition with its own degree of Muslim-Hindu assimilation. The *Nathpanthi yogis* are well known in the Shirdi region and the picture of their founders can be purchased at the Shirdi shrine."

Nathpanthi saints were famous for their *siddhis* (power to do miracles). Shirdi Sai Baba also had exhibited a number of such powers. *Shri Sai Sat Charita* and several other books on the life and miracles of

Sri Shirdi Sai Baba are full of numerous incidents in which Baba used His *siddhis* for the welfare of His devotees. Like Guru Gorakhnath, Shirdi Sai Baba was also using the ash (*udi* or *vibhuti*) of the *dhuni* established by Him to cure His devotees of all kinds of illnesses and miseries.

As Incarnation of Kabir

Sri Shirdi Sai Baba had revealed to one of His close devotees that in one of His several incarnations, He was Kabir, the famous saint of the *bhakti* (meditation) period of medieval Indian history. Kabir's teacher was Saint Ramanand of Varanasi. It is believed that the same Guru Ramanand was reborn as Guru Venkusha of Sailu under whose care and guidance Shirdi Sai Baba lived and imbibed spirituality from the age of 4 to 16 (1842 to 1854).

It is on record that while giving His evidence in a case related to a devotee before a Commission of Enquiry, Shirdi Sai Baba had stated that His creed or religion was Kabir. No one knows for sure whether Kabir was born a Hindu or a Muslim but he was a weaver by profession and his life and teachings are most inspiring.

In his article "Kabir : the Iconoclast", eminent scholar Dr. Gopal Singh has thrown this valuable light on the great saint:

> Such utter contempt Kabir shows for the rituals and superstitious beliefs and so devastating he is in his criticism of the age-old religious practices and dogmas, both Hindu and Muslim that one is in fact dazzled by the boldness of his spiritual insights and the freshness of metaphor.

> Kabir is the worshipper of one God, both absolute and manifest in his creation. He can be attained, he says, through pure conduct and meditation, but through no ritual is he pleased, nor by high caste or station. The realization comes through one's illumination within, and not by performing pilgrimages, or offering oblations, propitiating the *Brahmins* or the *Mullahs* or performing the Haj, or by repeating the text of the books considered sacred by the devout.

> He ridicules the superstitious beliefs with a ruthlessness unheard of in the mystic compositions of anyone before him:

> If one attains *yoga* by roaming about naked,
>   Then the deer in the woods would all be emancipated!
> If by close-cropping the hair, one becomes a *siddha*,
>   Then all the shorn sheep would find deliverance forthwith!

Spiritual Heredity

> O friend, if one were to be redeemed by celibacy,
> Then all the eunuchs would be in the highest state of bliss!
> They who bathe morning and evening (to wash off their sins)
> Are no better than frogs who live constantly in the water!

He makes no distinction between Hindus and Muslims and argues against the rituals of both as is evident from his following songs:

> Wherefrom have the Hindus come?
> Wherefrom the Mulims?
> Who created the two Paths?
> O man of evil intent, reflect this in your mind;
> Who, pray, is the creator of Heaven and Hell?

According to Kabir, it is the pure conduct which avails one in the end, and not the beliefs which one holds or practices.... It is through contentment, right conduct, truthful living and compassion that God is attained, not through falsehood, greed and violence.... The householder must observe the rules of moral conduct as much as a recluse foregoes desire and sensuous tastes.... The recluse or the devotee, however, is not to be denied his daily necessities; it is, therefore, in the fitness of things that Kabir demands from God all the wherewithals of a cultured life. He has no use for a God who keeps him famished and hungry, and yet demands devotion and dedication from him.

According to Kabir, "for the man who realises God, the distinctions of creed, caste or colour disappear and he sees the One alone in all." Kabir is thus the Guru of the modern enlightened world, which seeks to fight fundamentalism, superstition, but cannot and yet seek spiritual illumination and love for all.

Shirdi Sai Baba's teachings and style of functioning greatly resembled Kabir. It is of interest that in the *sakhis* and *dohas* of Kabir, the word "Sai" (meaning God) was used at some places. As a matter of fact, the earliest use of the word 'Sai' in Hindi language was found only in the compositions of Kabir.

Sai Baba's Dwarka Mai Masjid welcomed both Hindus and Muslims as well as others in a perfectly secular and tolerant manner. Like Kabir, Baba tried to teach the basics of sprirituality to all people in a plain, straightforward and simple manner. However, there was a difference : while Kabir ridiculed the established religious traditions and rituals like idol worship, reading of sacred texts, establishment of temples and mosques, traditional modes of worship, etc., Sai Baba did not do so. In the spirit of secularism and tolerance, He allowed His devotees to stick to their chosen gods and goddesses, traditional modes of worship and acts of charity like giving *dakshina* or *dan,* feeding the hungry and all such things. This prominently positive and integrative approach won for Him a unique veneration and love of people of all communities despite His often curt, impolite and abusive speech and His beating the devotees in moods of feigned anger. It may thus be said that Sai Baba was an improved model of Kabir suited to the socio-cultural context of the later half of the 19th century and the early two decades of the 20th century. The *siddhis* or miracle, making powers displayed by Him so frequently and effortlessly and boons given to barren women, diseased, poor and unfortunate people and deliverance from the cycle of birth and death to several people as well as animals and, above all, His frequent revelations about innumerable past births of men, women, children, creatures like snakes, frogs, dogs, buffaloes, tigers, etc., made Him all the more adorable, loving and far more impressive than His past incarnation as Kabir.

While Kabir emerged as a radical and iconoclastic spiritualist in the mould of a religious reformer, Sai Baba truly projected Himself as an all embracing, kind, bountiful, omnipresent, omnipotent and omniscient God eager to help His devotees of all faiths, materially as well as spiritually. While Kabir laid emphasis only on the *nirakar* (formless) God, Baba was more pragmatic than him, for He felt that the rural and traditional folk could comprehend the *nirakar* only after they had seen a *sakar* God in the form of statues as well as in the form of his Living personality as an incarnation of God.

Professor White, in the course of philosophical research on the Sai Baba movement, has tried to correlate *Nathpanthis,* Kabir and Sai Baba in a common bond of linkage. According to him:

> It is not known precisely whether he (Kabir) was born a Muslim or a Hindu but Charlotte Vaudeville is of the view that he belonged to a *jati* which had been converted from Hinduism to Islam in fairly recent times and had called themselves Yogis and lived a householder's life. Although a Hindu, apparently by choice, and a theist, he taught an extreme form of devotion to God without qualities; he also referred to God of his inner experience as the Guru. There is some evidence that he had been trained but had rejected the type of Yoga practised in the *Nathpanthi* order and there is even a tradition that he and Gorakhnath had met.... Kabir's humble origin, his love for all mankind whether Hindu, Muslim or otherwise, his reputed affection

Spiritual Heredity

for animals, his yogic connections (perhaps with the *Nathpanthi* order) and the uniquely synthetic character of his religious position point the direction toward the founder of the Sai Baba movement.

In *Shri Sai Sat Charita*, Hemadpant describes the well known incident of Baba grinding wheat in order to prevent cholera epidemic from affecting Shirdi. After describing that incident, the author recalls a similar story connected with Kabir:

> This reminds of a similar story of Kabir who seeing a woman grinding corn said to his guru, Nipathiranjan, "I am weeping because I feel the agony of being crushed in this wheel of worldly existence like the corn in the hand mill." Nipathiranjan replied, "Do not be afraid; hold fast to the handle of knowledge of this mill, as I do, and do not wander away from the same but turn inward to the centre, and you are sure to be saved."

Alongwith these interesting theories, it must be noted that Baba Himself disclosed that He was always present, His age was "lakhs of years", His caste or community was *Parvardigar* (God) and He had taken innumerable incarnations. He informed His devotee Shama that He had been with him for the last 74 births. He informed Narke and Hemadpant that He had been with them for the last 30 births. He told several other devotees about their past lives. He told a lady, Biyaja Bai Kote, that she had been His sister in many of her past births. Baba told one of His devotees that He had lived at Shirdi thousands of years earlier also and that His Guru's Samadhi was located under a particular *neem* tree. The non *Gurusthan* (Teacher's place) is there, which is venerated as a very holy spot in Shirdi by all devotees.

Baba's Other Incarnations
Baba once recalled one of His births in the fifteenth century when He was a Muslim *faqir* and had gone to meet a Brahmin Yogi, Mukund Brahamachari who did not welcome Him. Then at the market place, He saw a young royal couple, Humayun and his wife Hamida, in exile with three attendants. They were begging for water and the Faqir gave them water from His *kamandalu* (vessel), and blessed the couple that a son would be born to them and He would be a king of India. That child became Akbar. Mukund Brahamachari soon thereafter died and was reincarnated as Akbar, as per Baba's prophecy.

Baba once told His devotees, Khaparde and his wife, that both of them had contacts with each other in many previous lives. He told Khaparde that they had been kinsmen in a former life, had lived together for about two or three years, as wealthy persons, and after some years Khaparde had left His company and gone to a distant place to serve as a king.

Thus we can understand that Sai Baba has been appearing at different times and in many forms in His numerous incarnations during the last several thousand of years. Like the famed 'Babaji', Guru of Paramahansa Yogananda's Guru, Lahri Mahasahay, He has been present on this earth constantly in various forms.

I am the mother — origin of all beings — the Harmony of the three gunas, the Propeller of all senses, the Creator, Preserver and Destroyer.
—Sri Shirdi Sai Baba

3
Origin

THERE are two popular sayings in our country:

"A Sadhu has no caste".
"One should not try to find the origin of a river or a saint".

It is true that it is far more important for us to know the message or contribution of great saints than to know about their family history, circumstances of birth, etc. But as human beings with curiosity as one of our basic instincts, we cannot resist the temptation or curiosity of trying to discover the family background and circumstances of the birth of saints.

When Sri Shirdi Sai Baba was alive (1838 - 1918), no one actually knew or could tell with any measure of authority about the parentage, circumstances of birth and early childhood of Baba. The villagers of Shirdi and the contemporary devotees could not say with certainty whether Baba was a Hindu or a Muslim. Baba Himself did not disclose it as He did not want His devotees to bother about knowing His backgrond. He was more concerned about the establishment of Hindu-Muslim unity and about the welfare and spiritual elevation of His devotees, rather than establishing and promoting a personality for Himself.

However, the testimonies of some of His close devotees like Mlahaspati, Abdul, Das Ganu, Shama, Sai Sharananandji, etc., reveal that Baba had certainly given a number of crucial hints very casually about His origin and early childhood. The following hints given by Him are thus relevant:

i) An extract from *Shri Sai Sat Charita:*

Mlahaspati, an intimate devotee of Shirdi Sai Baba, who always slept with Him in the *masjid* and *chavadi*, said that Sai Baba told him that He was a Brahmin of Pathri and was handed over to a *faqir* in His infancy. When He told this, some men from Pathri had come and Baba was enquiring about some people from that place.

Mrs. Kashibai Kanitkar, the famous learned woman of Poona, says in one of the experiences published in *Sai Leela*:

On hearing of Baba's miracles, we were discussing according to our theosophic convention and fashion whether Sai Baba belonged to the Black or White Lodge. When once I went to Shirdi, I was thinking seriously about this in my mind. As soon as I approached the steps of the *masjid*, Baba came to the front and pointing to His chest and staring at me spoke rather vehemently — "This is a Brahmin, pure Brahmin. He has nothing to do with black things. No Musalman can dare step in here. He dare not." Again pointing to His chest, he said "This Brahmin alone can bring lakhs on the white path and take them to their destination. This is a Brahmin's *masjid* and I won't allow any black Mohamedan to cast His shadow here."

ii) Baba told Sharananand also in 1912 that He was a Brahmin.

iii) In his testimony, Das Ganu, a close devotee of Baba, stated that Baba had revealed the following facts about Him to Nana Joshi, Commissioner sent by Dhulia Court to Baba to examine Him in a trial case concerning a thief who had been charged with the theft of jewels:

Commissioner (C): What is your Name?

Baba (B): They call me Sai Baba.

C: Your father's name?

B: Also Sai Baba.

C: Your Guru's name?

B: Venkusha.

C: Creed or Religion?

B: Kabir.

C: Caste or Race?

B: Parvardigar (God).

Origin

iv) *Shri Sai Sat Charita* records Mrs. Radhabai Deshmukh's experience. Baba once told her:

I resorted to my Guru for 12 years. He brought me up. There was no dearth of food and clothing. He was full of love, nay He was love incarnate. How can I describe it? I loved Him the most. Rare is a Guru like him.

v) Early in October 1918, Baba's most favourite possession, a brick, which was His Guru's parting gift to Him in 1854 fell down from the hands of the boy, Madhav Fasle, in Dwarka Mai Masjid and broke. Baba was very much depressed to see it and said, "It is not the brick that is broken; it is my destiny. It has been my lifelong companion and I meditated on the self with its help; it is my very life. It has left me today. I shall not survive for long."

vi) *Shri Sai Sat Charita* also records this incident:

In 1916, on the Vijayadashmi (Dussehra) Baba suddenly got into wild rage in the evening when people were returning from 'Seemallanghan' (crossing the border or limits of the village). Taking off His headdress, *kafni* and *langota,* etc., He tore them and threw them in the *dhuni* before them. Fed by this offering, the fire in the *dhuni* began to burn brighter and Baba shone still brighter. He stood there stark naked and with His burning red eyes shouted, "You fellows, now have a look and decide finally whether I am a Moslem or a Hindu.

The devotees looked at the Baba and found that He had not been circumcised and, therefore, He was not a Muslim but a Hindu. It was also discovered by Baba's devotees that His earlobes had been pierced as is the custom in the Hindus.

vii) Baba had once told His devotees that He was given to a *faqir* by His parents in His childhood. These hints had given the broad idea to most of His contemporary devotees that Baba was a Brahmin by birth and was trained under a Brahmin Guru Venkusha, but they did not know anything more than this.

During the last two decades, three valuable sources of information about Sri Shirdi Baba's origin and childhood have emerged:

1) Research findings of V. N. Kher.
2) Revelations of Sri Sathya Sai Baba, the incarnation of Sri Shirdi Sai Baba.

3) Recently published memoirs of Shivamma Thayee, 104 years old lady, the only surviving devotee of Shirdi Sai Baba.

Research Findings of V. N. Kher

V. N. Kher, a noted Gandhian and an ardent Sai devotee, went to Pathri village in 1975 to discover the facts of Shirdi Sai Baba's family background. He did extensive investigations contacting each Brahmin family in the village. He had detailed discussions with one Professor Raghunath Bhusari, a retired Professor of Marathi at the Osmania University, Hyderabad, who was believed to be a member of Shirdi Sai Baba's clan.

Kher's research findings are:

i) The Brahmins of Pathri are all Desatha Brahmins — either Rigvedi or Yajurvedi; there are no Brahmins of any other sub-caste.

ii) The family deity of almost all the Brahmin families of Pathri is either Goddess Renuka Mahur or Yogeswari of Ambajogai. There is only one exception, that of Bhusari family whose family deity is Hanuman of Kumhar-bavadi on the outskirts of Pathri village.

iii) Kuner Dada was the first known ancestor of this Bhusari clan of Brahmins of Pathri. No information was available about the next two generations. Then there was one Parsuram. He had five sons — Raghupati, Dada, Haribhau, Ambadas and Balwant. Haribhau, Ambadas and Balwant had left Pathri for good. Haribhau might have gone in search of God, while the other two went to seek their fortunes elsewhere.

iv) In all probability, Haribhau Bhusari later on became known as Sai Baba of Shirdi.

v) The House (No. 4-438-6I) in Vaishnav Gali near Kumhar-bavadi in Pathri village, which was in ruins when V. B. Kher visited it in 1975, was identified as the family house of Sai Baba. This has now been taken over by the local Sai Samiti for Shirdi Sai Temple where prayers are held every Thursday.

Kher's findings certainly are interesting. One of the most important findings that Sai Baba's clan worshipped Hanuman has great significance. In the course of our own research on Sri Shirdi Sai Baba, we have discovered the following evidence:

a) It has been reported by several devotees who had seen Baba that He used to pay special regards to Hanuman.

Origin 23

b) In His early years at Shirdi (1958-78) Baba used to visit Maruti (Hanuman) Temple close to His Dwarka Mai Masjid so very often and meet saint Devidas who used to live there, and the two used to talk for hours.

c) Baba had got the Maruti Temple renovated at His own cost and inspiration.

d) While going to *Chavadi* every alternate evening and while returning from *Chavadi* to Dwarka Mai Masjid the next morning, in the procession, Baba used to stop for a moment, look invariably towards the Hanuman (Maruti) Temple and make some mysterious spiritual gestures towards it. This has been reported by a number of contemporary devotees.

e) Baba's love and regards for Hanuman and Rama were well known to most of His contemporary devotees.

Sathya Sai Baba's Revelation about Shirdi Sai Baba

Sri Sathya Sai Baba of Puttaparthi (Andhra Pradesh) disclosed, when he was a boy of 14, on 23rd May, 1940, that He was Sai Baba — reincarnation of Sri Shirdi Sai Baba. He is accepted as the incarnation of Sri Shirdi Sai Baba by millions of devotees throughout the world.

In 1974, Sri Sathya Sai Baba revealed some unknown facts about the birth and childhood of Sri Shirdi Sai Baba's incarnation and His own previous life to Professor V. K. Gokak, Professor S. Bhagvantam and some others. Professor Gokak recorded those revelations in his *Foreword* to T. S. Anantha Murthy's book *Life and Teachings of Sri Sai Baba of Shirdi* (1974). Gokak's account of what Sri Sathya Sai Baba told him and others in 1974 about Sri Shirdi Sai Baba's birth and childhood are reproduced below:

> Sai Baba of Shirdi was the third child of a boatman, Ganga Bavadia, who lived in Pathri, a village near Manmad, on the banks of a river. His (Sri Sai Baba's) mother's name was Devagiriamma. On a certain night when the river was in spate, the boatman Ganga Bavadia, who had all his boats moored to the bank, was scared that they might be swept away by the swirling waters. He went to the riverside, leaving his wife alone at home. At that time, an old man came and asked Devagiriamma to give him food. She served him food in the verandah.
>
> He then asked for permission to sleep there as he had nowhere to go. She permitted him to sleep in the verandah. After a little while, she

heard somebody tapping at the door. It was the old man again. He said that he could not sleep. He desired that a lady should massage his legs. Devagiriamma went at that hour of the night by the back door to the houses of one or two courtesans, but could not find any of them at home. She was bewildered and did not know what to do. She was a devotee of Goddess Parvati and her husband was a devotee of *Easwara* (Shiva). She sat in her worship-room and prayed and cried bitterly.

At that moment, she heard a knock on the back-door. As she opened the door, she saw a woman standing there who said that she was from one of those houses that Devagiriamma had visited and she wanted to know what could she do for her. Devagiriamma was overcome with joy and she took the woman to the old man in the verandah and closed the door on both of them. After a while, she heard another tap on the verandah door. She thought that the woman probably wanted to return home, so she opened the door. What did she see there? Lord Shiva and Goddess Parvati were themselves standing there, ready to bless her.

Goddess Parvati said to Shiva, "Let us together bless her." Shiva replied, "Since I came here to test her, I will speak to her separately." Devagiriamma was childless till then. Goddess Parvati blessed her and said, "Be the mother of two children." Devagiriamma bowed to Shiva, who said to her, "I will be born as your third child, a son." By the time Devagiriamma looked up, the Divine pair had vanished.

When the husband (Ganga Bavadia) came home in the early hours of the morning, Devagiriamma narrated all her strange experiences to him. He was incredulous and thought it all to be the result of an over-heated brain, as she had been left alone at home on a stormy night. But the events that followed did prove the veracity of her experiences. Devagiriamma became the mother of two children and it was soon clear that she would become the mother of a third child also.

But an unusual situation developed on the domestic front. The husband gradually lost all his interest in mundane things and was pining to meet God face to face. When his wife reminded him all that the Divine couple had told her had come true and Shiva himself would now be born as their child, he said, "Even if it be so, it will not satisfy me. There will be the mask of human child between me and

Origin

God. I want to seek that unmitigated primordial splendour," and set out on his quest. Torn between her husband and her children, Devagiriamma decided that it was her duty to follow her husband in his footsteps, so she sent her two children to her mother's home and accompanied her husband into the forest.

After they had covered some distance, Devagiriamma felt that she was soon going to give birth to a child because the birthpains had started. She implored her husband to wait for a while, but he kept going his way. As soon as she was delivered of the baby boy, beneath the shade of a banyan tree, she placed her child on the ground, covered it with banyan leaves and hastened after her husband, for her duty lay in that direction. Bloodstains were still visible on the child's tender body and one could make out that it was born only a few minutes earlier.

This is how destiny works. A person named 'Patil' from a neighbouring village was fetching his wife from her mother's hamlet, in a *tonga* (horse carriage). At that very spot, his wife felt like answering a call of nature. Mr. Patil asked the tonga-driver to stop for a while.

Mrs. Patil alighted from the *tonga* and went to the very spot where the child had been made to lie by Devagiriamma. She heard the child's cry, removed the leaves and found that it was a newborn child. Excited, she called her husband to the spot and showed him the child. They were a childless couple and it was their feeling that God had blessed them with this child. They took the child home and brought it up as their own son.

On 28 September, 1990, and then on 27 September 1992, Sri Sathya Sai Baba gave two full-fledged discourses on the life of Sri Shirdi Sai Baba. In these discourses, He repeated almost all the above account and added the following facts of great interest:

1) Devagiriamma had mixed some flour with curds and given it as food to the old man (Lord Shiva).

2) Parvathi then blessed her (Devagiriamma): "I grant you a son to maintain the lineage and a daughter for *kanya-ka-dan* (a girl to be offered in marriage)."

3) She (Devagiriamma) was delivered of the boy. Wrapping the baby in a piece of cloth, she left the child by the roadside and followed her husband.

4) This day (the first day of *Navaratri*) has another significance : Shirdi Sai Baba was born on 27 September, 1938.

An analysis of all the reliable facts provide us the following conclusions:

i) To some extent, the information given by V.B. Kher about Sri Shirdi Sai Baba's parentage seems to be correct, particularly the one that Baba's parents were Desatha Yajurvedi Brahmins whose family deity was Hanuman of Kumhar-bavadi on the outskirts of Pathri village.

ii) Kher has stated that Parsuram had five sons and the third one 'Haribhau' was perhaps the one who later became Sai Baba of Shirdi. But Sri Sathya Sai Baba mentioned Ganga Bavadia as the father of Shirdi Sai Baba, and added that after the birth of one son and one daughter Shirdi Sai Baba was born to Devagiriamma, wife of Ganga Bavadia.

a) It is possible that Parsuram might have been the childhood name and Ganga the adulthood name of Shirdi Sai Baba's father. It is customary in Hindu families to change one's childhood name when a boy or girl becomes somewhat grown up and starts going out.

b) It is likely that Raghupati and Dada might be names of the two children who died in their infancy in the early years of married life of Devagiriamma. Then three children including the youngest one Haribhau might have been born to her as per boons granted to her by Shakti and Shiva. Kher mentions the names Haribhau, Ambadas, Balwant; perhaps instead of them and in that order, the three later children of Devagiriamma were Ambadas, a girl (maybe Balwant Bai or so) and Haribhau. If this is correct, then one can say that the findings of Kher and revelations of Sri Sathya Sai Baba come very close as real facts. At any rate, we are inclined to believe in what Sri Sathya Sai Baba has revealed.

c) Kher's finding that Sri Shirdi Sai Baba belonged to Bhusari family of Pathri to which Professor Raghunath Bhusari belongs and the surname 'Bhavadia' of Baba's father Ganga can be accepted. Actually, it should be 'Bavadia' i.e., one who lives near a *bavadi* (natural water pond) in a village. Kher has mentioned that Sai Baba's ancestral family lived in a house near *Kumhar Bavadi* (the pond of the Kumhars, i.e., potters), and were the worshippers of Hanuman whose temple was located there.

Origin

d) On the basis of these circumstantial evidences, we may assume that in all probability the child was born at or near noon, say between 12 noon and 1.30 p.m. or so. The reasons for estimating the time of birth to be near the noon are that the parents of Baba might have left their house in Pathri early in the morning of 27 September, 1838 at about 5 a.m. or so; they might have covered the distance of 4-5 miles on foot by say 11 a.m., since Devagiriamma, was in a very advanced stage of pregnancy; *Faqir* Patil and his wife *Faqiri* might have reached that spot in the forest at or slightly after 12 noon, since it is customary in the Indian families to allow a married girl and her husband to leave the girl's parental home only after lunch. They should have covered a distance of 7-8 miles through the forest in about 2 hours. If they left Patil's house after lunch at about 10 a.m. they might have reached that spot near the banyan tree in the forest around 1 p.m. Based on these assumptions, it would be fair to assess that Baba's birth time should be about 12 noon or so, some 40 to 50 minutes before the arrival of Patil's *tonga*. It is only Sri Sathya Sai Baba, the present re-incarnation of Shirdi Sai Baba, who can, if He so wishes, enlighten the world by revealing the exact time and planetary positions of Shirdi Sai Baba's birth.

"If one meditates on Me, repeats My name, sings My deeds, and is thus transformed in Me, one's Karma is destroyed. I stay by his side always.

—Sri Shirdi Sai Baba

4

Childhood

PROF. V. K. Gokak, on information from Sri Sathya Sai Baba in 1974, revealed the following about Sri Shirdi Sai Baba's childhood at *faqir* Patil's house which was in Manwat village.

The child grew up in the Patil household. Patil died when the child was growing into boyhood. The mother was the one left to take care of Him. She was unable to cope with His activities. The boy used to go to Hindu temples and recite the *Quran* there. He installed a stone *lingam* in a mosque and worshipped it there. Enraged Hindu and Muslim neighbours came to the foster-mother and complained bitterly about the boy. She was puzzled.

One day, the boy was playing marbles with the son of a neighbouring *sahukar* or a wealthy man. The *sahukar's* son lost all his marbles to Baba (Shirdi Sai Baba as a boy). Tempted by the game, the *sahukar's* son went to his mother's worship room, seized a *saligram* or a black globular stone kept there for worship and played with it with Babu. The *sahukar's* son lost that *saligram* also to Baba; but he thought that Babu had played foul and the *saligram* should be returned to him. Babu refused to part with it. He kept it in His mouth. The *sahukar's* son went to his mother, told her how he had taken the *saligram* away from her prayer room and played with it as a marble and that Babu had taken it away through foul play.

Horrified, the *sahukar's* wife rushed to her prayer room and found that the *saligram* was missing. She ran to Babu who was standing

Childhood

with her son outside and importuned Him to return the *saligram*. Babu sat tight-lipped and refused to return it. She then compelled Babu to open His mouth and saw in it what Yashoda had seen in Sri Krishna's mouth — the *Vishwarupa* (worlds rolling on worlds). Babu laughingly said that the *saligram* was in the prayer room. She ran back to Babu and prostrated herself before Him. She had now realised that He was divine. Thereafter, she went to Babu's house every day to touch His feet. It was only when people criticised her about it that she turned this homage into a mental act.

But Babu's disturbing acts — His Hindu worship in mosques and Muslim in temples — continued to irritate the people. Unable to control the boy, Mrs. Patil, the foster-mother, came to know of an *ashram*, started some miles away by a *sadhu* named Venkusha. There were in the *ashram* some orphan boys and waifs. She decided to take Babu and leave him there.

Venkusha had a dream the night previous to the arrival of the foster-mother with Babu. In this dream, Lord Shiva told Venkusha that He, (Shiva) would go to Venkusha the next morning about 1 a.m. and sure enough, Mrs. Patil went there at about that time, with Babu. She told Venkusha about the boy's disturbing activities and prayed to Venkusha to take Babu as an inmate of the *ashram*. Venkusha did so with great delight and veneration.

Venkusha was extremely fond of Babu. He showered all his affections on Babu who became an object of jealousy for the other boys and they were bent on persecuting Him. They got the opportunity one morning when Venkusha sent Babu to bring some *bilva* leaves for worship. As Babu went into the woods, he was overtaken by a group of the other boys. They beat Him up and threw a brick at Him. It hit him on the forehead. He bled profusely. Babu did not say a word. He picked up the brick, which had some bloodstains on it and returned to Venkusha. Venkusha was deeply grieved to see Babu in this plight. He tore a *dhoti* (loin cloth) and dressed the forehead wound, bandaging it round the forehead. He shed tears over the brick that had been thrown at Babu. He kept it with himself for it was stained with the blood of *Eeswara* Himself. There is, in Sri Sai Baba's biography a reference to the brick.

In his recent discourses of 28 September, 1990 and 27 September, 1992, Sri Sathya Sai Baba has made some further revelations about the childhood of Sri Shirdi Sai Baba:

i) "In those days, Hindu-Muslim differences in that area were growing alarmingly. There was considerable bitterness between members of the two communities. What the boy (Babu) used to do was to visit a Hindu temple and sing songs in praise of Allah saying *"Mein Allah hoon!"* (I am God); *"Allah Malik Hai"* (God is the Supreme Lord). The Hindus used to chastise the boy in various ways for His behaviour. Nor was that all for He would enter a mosque and declare: "Rama is God," "Shiva is *Allah.*" His behaviour in singing about Rama and Shiva in a mosque was a puzzle to the public. Members belonging to both the communities went to the Faqir's wife and complained about the boy's behaviour".

ii) "As He (child Babu) was a foundling, the *faqir* (Patil) had no natural affection for him."

At this stage, facts revealed by the research of V.N. Kher and the two somewhat related popular folk stories narrated by Kher and Shivamma Thayee separately can be taken note of.

According to Kher's research:

1) Gopal Rao Deshmukh *nee* 'Venkusha' was the ruler or prince of the *Jagir* (estate) of paragana. He was a humble, kind and merciful man who possessed powers to cure diseases and had to his credit eight *mahasiddhis* (attainment of powers by deep and at times prolonged meditation) — *Anima, Mahima, Laghima, Prapti, Prakaashya, Ishitaa, Vashita, Yatkaa, Stadasyati.* He lived in Sailu near Pathri and ran an *ashram* at his big house.

2) Venkusha was Kabir's Guru Ramanand in his previous life when Sri Sai Baba was Kabir. There was a legend that once he went to Ahmedabad to visit the *dargah* (tomb) of Suva Shah. As he entered it, the tomb perspired and burst into speech, saying, *"Salaam Alekum* — Oh, you great sage Ramanand, in your present birth truly you have not forgotten me, even though you have changed your form and appear before me as a Deshmukh in the Moghalai (Nizam's Dominion). From the town of Manwat, ten miles from Sailu, your former disciple, Kabir, will come to you as a child of a *faqir.*" The caretaker of the *dargah* also heard the words and wondered at them.

As prophesied, the wife of the Faqir of Manwat came to Sailu to see Gopalrao. She was an oldish woman in her fifties and was clad in rags. She wore green bangles on her wrists and carried a boy of five, who Gopalrao guessed was Kabir of his previous birth.

Childhood

...The boy immediately recognised his master of a previous birth and sought refuge in him. Both, the woman and her child were provided shelter by Gopalrao.... When the boy was twelve, his (foster) mother died.

The popular folk tale recorded by Kher states that the brick had hit Guru Venkusha in the jungle when both Baba and Venkusha had gone there for meditation. However, Sri Sathya Sai Baba's revelation discards this part of the story.

The popular story recorded by Kher and the one recalled by Shivamma Thayee, however, agree on one point that soon after the brick incident, Guru Venkusha wished to transfer all his spiritual powers to Babu and so he asked Him to go and fetch milk of a cow and that too a black one. The only black cow available in the nearby herd was barren and yielded no milk. Kher says that Babu reported this to Venkusha, so Venkusha came there and by his touching the cow's udders, milk came out. Shivamma's story, however, tells us that Baba (Babu) Himself touched the udders of the cow and milk came out of them. Anyway, when the milk (some 3 seers) of the cow was brought by Baba (Babu) before Venkusha, the latter asked Him to drink the whole of it. Kher says, "The master gathered three seers of creamy milk and handed it over to the boy. He then removed the piece of cloth covering His own head and tied it round the boy's head saying, "I have given you my entire wealth. The three seers of milk given to you are *karma*, *bhakti*, (meditation) and *jnana* (wisdom). I have sanctified the milk, hence drink it up and you will get *jnana*."

Both stories also agree on the point that the boy who had hurled the brick had died instantaneously. When the news of death was brought to Venkusha and Babu by a boy, on Venkusha's instructions, Babu immediately went to the dead boy, touched him and made him alive. Venkusha gave a loin cloth to Baba, advised him to leave the place immediately and go towards Godavari river (towards Shirdi). Soon thereafter, he entered *Maha Samadhi*.

Kamath and Kher have cast doubts on the popular belief that Venkusha was the *Guru* of Sri Shirdi Sai Baba. According to them, Venkusha had died in 1802 and his tomb was erected in 1808 behind Venkateshwar Temple, about half a mile from Sailu railway station, and it was thus much before the birth of Sri Shirdi Sai Baba.

Sai Sharnananda has stated in his book *Sri Sai The Superman* that Baba had told him, "My Guru's name is Roshan Shah Mian." According to him, "Subsequently I marked that Shri Baba was from time to time also using the word 'Roshan'. He used it particularly when telling some parables."

"...one should not be astonished that Roshan Shah of whom Baba often spoke did exist in flesh and blood and Baba devotedly served him for over twelve years. It seems that Roshan Shah cast off his mortal coil — his body — and Baba entombed him under or near the *neem* tree still existing in the Shirdi *Vavalkar Vada*."

These statements of Kamath and Kher and Sai Sharnananda cast doubt on the fact of Venkusha being the Guru of Baba. However, Sri Shirdi Sai Baba Himself in His testimony before the Court Commisioner, Joshi had testified that His Guru was Venkusha. Sri Sathya Sai Baba also revealed the facts as to how Babu reached Venkusha's *ashram* at Sailu, lived there for 12 years (from 1842 to 1854) and how He left it one evening in 1854 and reached Shirdi. In view of the foregoing, these facts have to be accepted and those of Kamath and Kher as well as Sai Sharnananda's statements have to be discarded. Since Baba used to speak of previous lives also and often told many things in parables, it is possible that Roshan Mian might have been Baba's Guru in a previous birth in Shirdi; He was certainly different from Guru Venkusha of Sailu with whom Baba lived from 1842 to 1854. This was also corroborated by a famous saint Sakha Ram Maharaj, who was also a *Gurubhai* (colleague) of Baba at Guru Venkusha's *ashram* at Sailu during these years.

I am the bonded slave of My devotees. I love devotion. ...As soon a devotee calls unto Me with love, I will appear. I require no train to travel.

—Sri Shirdi Sai Baba

5
Sojournings

Events of 1854
AFTER leaving His Guru's *ashram,* one evening in early 1854, most probably after *Shivaratri* in February 1854, Babu, the young saint, attired as a Muslim *faqir* with a *kafni* (headdress) walked by foot all alone with the brick and loin cloth gifted to Him by Venkusha.

It seems that He did not go to Shirdi directly. The following disclosure by Baba to His devotees, Bade Baba and Bapugir Gasavi, as recorded by Gawankar, is revealing:

> I grew up (lived) in Mahugarh (a holy place of Lord Dattatreya); when people pestered Me I left for Girnar, there too people troubled Me much, so I left for Mount Abu (in Rajasthan). There too the same thing happened. Then I came to Akkalkot and from there to Daulatabad. Then Janardana Swami (a great saint) did Me a lot of *seva* (service). Then I went to Pandharpur; from there I came to Shirdi.

This shows that Baba first of all reached Mahugarh from Sailu and stayed there for some weeks. It also shows that He must have taken months in going to so many places, so He might have in all probability reached Shirdi in September 1854 or so.

First Visit to Shirdi
Baba reached Shirdi as a 16-year-old handsome boy attired as a Muslim *faqir.* He perhaps wanted to stay in Khandoba Temple, but out of orthodoxy, the priest of that temple, Mlahaspati, did not allow Him to do

so. So He took shelter under a *neem* tree outside Shirdi village on the other side of the Khandoba Temple which was an isolated place near a jungle of *babul* shrubs at that time.

He dug out a pit at the foot of the *neem* tree and for most of the time sat hidden in that pit. Baba later on disclosed that He had been undergoing penance or meditation in that pit, the passage from which led to a long dark cave. He lived the life of a recluse, seldom visible to people. The first person to see Him was Mlahaspati who felt attracted by His magnetic, youthful and silent personality and also got His two close friends, Kashinath Sipmi (a tailor and a cloth merchant) and Jogle, interested in the young *faqir*. One peasant couple, Appa Patil Kote and his wife Bayjabai who met Him, were also very much impressed by His Godly personality. Bayjabai then and there decided to take up the vow of giving Him *roti* at lunch every day and herself eating her lunch only after that. She used to search for the young *faqir* (who never disclosed His name) in the nearby fields and jungle and feed Him with motherly love.

The young *faqir* sometimes begged for food in the village — once, twice or more, or sometimes not at all. Sai Sharananand has written that Baba had disclosed to him in 1910, "He used to live under that *neem* tree all alone doing penance as the tomb of one of His previous lives was located there. After years of such penance in the cave, people caught sight of Him one day when He came out for water. It seemed He had finished His tenure of penance because thereafter He did not return to the cave."

This statement of Sai Sharnanandji seems to be somewhat incorrect. How could Baba do penance for years under that tree when He had actually stayed in Shirdi for hardly two months in 1854? Perhaps Baba might have referred to His penance in that very cave under that very *neem* tree, in one of His previous lives for 12 years in the presence of His Guru 'Roshan Shah' who was a Muslim saint. .

There exists a recorded testimony describing the 16 years old young Baba under that *neem* tree in 1854: Nana Chopdar's mother, an old lady, saw this young *faqir* one day and she portrayed Him in these words:

> This young lad, fair, smart and very handsome, was first seen under the *neem* tree, seated in *asana* (yogic posture). The people of the village were wonderstruck to see such a young lad practising hard penance, not minding heat and cold. By day he associated with none, by night he was afraid of none.... Outwardly he looked very young

Sojournings 35

but by his actions He was really a great soul. He was the embodiment of dispassion and was an enigma to all.

The young *faqir* told Mlahaspati and His friends decided that the place where He stayed under the *neem* tree, being the tomb of His Guru of previous birth, was a sacred place and so it should be kept safe, clean, plastered with cowdung, and *loban* (incense) should be burnt on it. Mlahaspati and His friends agreed to do so. Assuring them thus, one night He slipped out of Shirdi without informing anybody. He had stayed there hardly for two months.

Events During 1854 - 1858
It seems that Baba left Shirdi in November 1854 or so. What He did during his *agyatvas* (period of disguised wanderings) of about three and a half or four years, i.e. till 1958, is still shrouded in mystery. However, a close perusal of *Sri Sai Sat Charita, Devotees, Experiences of Sri Sai Baba,* Khaparde's *Shirdi Diary* and some other valuable books have enabled us to discover some of the valuable hints given by Baba to some of His close devotees with regard to the events of His life during these four mysterious years, and on that basis, the order of those events can be reconstructed as under:

i) On 30 December, 1911, Shirdi Sai Baba told some devotees including Khaparde that He had stayed at Aurangabad with a *faqir* for some time. Khaparde recorded it in his *Shirdi Diary* as under:

He (Sri Sai Baba) said He went to Aurangabad in one of His wanderings and saw a *faqir* sitting in a *masjid* near which there was a very tall *tarmind* tree. The *faqir* did not allow Him to enter the *masjid* at first but ultimately consented to His putting up in it. The *faqir* depended entirely on a piece of *roti* (cake) which an old woman used to supply him at midday. He (Baba) volunteered to beg for him and kept him supplied amply with food four years and then thought of leaving the place. The old *faqir* shed tears and had to be consoled with soft words. Sai Maharaj visited him four years later and found him there doing well. The *faqir* then came here (Shirdi) a few years ago and lodged at *Chawdi*. From what he said I gathered that Sai Baba stayed twelve years to instruct the Aurangabad *faqir* and set him up fully in the spiritual world.

It seems that the *faqir* with whom Baba stayed in the Aurangabad mosque and served him was Bade Baba or *faqir* Meer Mohammad Yasin Mian or Malegaon Baba *faqir*, who had in his very old age come to stay with Sri Sai Baba at Shirdi and whom Baba used to give the highest amount of daily gift out of His day's collection of *dakshina* (alms) from visitors and devotees. Baba met him after four years, which means He visited him at Aurangabad again in 1858 some weeks before His reaching Shirdi. It, however, appears that Khaparde also perhaps did not hear or understand the Baba's revelation correctly. Baba might have mentioned just 'twelve' or 'twelve months', not 'twelve years', for how could He stay at Aurangabad for 12 years when the duration between His two visits to Shirdi was just less than four years?

ii) It is evident from the following disclosure by Baba to some of the devotees that He worked for about 10-12 months in 1856:

> When I was a youngster, I was in search of bread and butter and went to Badgaum. There I got an embroidery work. I worked hard, sparing no pains. The employer was very much pleased with me. Three other boys had worked before me. The first got Rs. 50/-, the second Rs. 100/- and I was given twice the whole of this amount. Seeing my cleverness, the employer presented me with a full dress, a turban for the head and a *shella* for the body, etc. I kept this dress intact without using it. I thought that what a man might give does not last long and is imperfect but what my *Sircar* (God) gives lasts to the end of time.

iii) Baba casually disclosed to Upasani Maharaj's elder brother on his first visit to Shirdi on 31 December, 1911 that He had been at the battle in which the Rani of Jhansi took part. He was then in the army. It is widely known that Rani Laxmi Bai of Jhansi was an important leader of the First War of India's Independence in 1857. She had fought against the British rulers of India and laid her life in the battle. It is possible that Baba under some other name might have been employed as a casual soldier in the army of Rani Laxmi Bai at Jhansi, or in one of her army units fighting the British near Aurangabad, Nagpur or Khandwa. However, Sholapurkar in *Footprints at Shirdi and Puttaparthi* has conjectured that He might have joined the army of Nana Saheb Peshwa at Bithur (near Kanpur) in Uttar Pradesh, who was an ally of Rani Laxmi Bai, but this does not appear to be correct. Most probably, Baba was employed in the army of Rani Jhansi which was fighting one of the battles with the British in the vicinity of Jhansi itself in 1857. After the martyrdom of Rani Jhansi, her army got disbanded, and Baba might have left the army and again donned His earlier dress and lifestyle of a Muslim *faqir* in order to hide His identity as an erstwhile soldier of the Rani Jhansi's army.

iv) He might have then visited on foot His native place passing through Pathri, the village of His birth, Sailu, the place of His Guru Venkusha's *ashram* and other places. This is evident from the following disclosure by Baba to some of His contemporary devotees:

> The path is from Pathri. From there Shillud (Sailu), Manoor (Manvat) and Jalnapur. I had been once (by that route). It took Me eight days. By day I trod over the grass and slept at night in the grass. We walked step by step.

Kamath and Kher here add that 'Thus Baba reached Paithan-Aurangabad' where He stayed for twelve years in a mosque and guided a *faqir*.

The first half of the above statement is correct, but the other half is totally incorrect. Baba certainly revisited Bade Baba at the Mosque at Paithan in Aurangabad in 1857 or early 1858 to enquire about his welfare, as Baba's revelation to Khaparde on 30 December, 1911 shows. He might have stayed there with him for a few days, but His stay there for twelve years is certainly incorrect.

v) Then we come across a valuable testimony of a businessman of Rahata Amool Chand Sait (Seth), with whose elder cousin, Khushal Chand, Baba later developed great friendship:

> My elder cousin Kushal Bhav, who died on 5-11-1918, told me that previously Sai Baba lived with a Muslim saint Ali (Akbar Ali perhaps) whose portrait is kept in our *gin*, i.e. *Rahatekar Gin* near Wadia Park at Ahmednagar, and Dalu Sait (son of Kushal Chand Sait) had seen Baba with the saint at Ahmednagar and that Baba came from Ahmednagar to live at Rahata and then went to live at Shirdi.

This evidence shows that Baba lived for some time — maybe for a few months — with the Muslim *faqir* Akbar Ali at Ahmednagar in 1858, but the latter part of the evidence 'that Baba came to live at Rahata and then went to live at Shirdi' does not seem to be in order.

vi) After leaving Ahmednagar, Baba was wandering. One day, He was seated under a *mango* tree by the side of the path in the forest near the twin villages of Bindhon-Sindhon, 24 kms from Aurangabad. Here Chand Bhai Patil (Patel), a well-off resident of Dhoop Kheda village, met Him (young *Faqir* Sai Baba). Chand Bhai was wandering with a horse saddle on his shoulders and seemed to be tired and worried. Baba called him by name and greatly impressed him as a divine personality by doing three miracles within a few minutes — showing his lost mare grazing under a tree nearby in the forest, materialising live embers from the ground by thrusting His *tongs*, and materialising water then and there for wetting the piece of cloth needed for smoking His *chilam* (clay pipe). This thrilling incident of the meeting of Chand Bhai Patil with the young Baba in 1858 is very widely mentioned in all books on Sai Baba and the Hindi Film *Shirdi Ke Sai Baba*.

vii) In some books, it is mentioned that on Chand Bhai's request, Baba went with him to his village Dhoopkheda on the same day. In some other books, it is metioned that Baba did not go with him on that very day, but He said that He would reach his village after 2-3 days. The latter seems to be correct for Chand Bhai did not ever tell anyone at Shirdi during his lifetime that Baba rode His mare alongwith him on His return journey to Dhoop Kheda. Kamath and Kher are of the view that Baba reached Dhoopkheda all alone after a few days to accept the hospitality of a grateful new devotee, Chand Bhai Patil; this seems to be perfectly correct.

Sholapurkar has recorded this thrilling incident of Baba's visit to Dhoopkheda as follows:

> When Baba went to Dhoop Kheda alongwith Chand Bhai, He threw stones at the advancing crowd who would not allow the two to proceed further. This behaviour of the crowd threw Baba in tantrums and He hurled stones all round. The crowd became panicky and ran helter-skelter. A stone, however, hit a small boy who was lame. The agonised mother ran to his rescue, but when she picked up the boy, there were no marks of injury or bleeding. On the contrary, the lameness was gone and the boy could walk normally. In another case, a stone hit a young girl, who moved about naked, being of unsound mind. The stone hit her on the forehead. Her mother ran to her rescue, but the girl ran past her and disappeared in the house and hurriedly put on a saree to cover her nakedness. Gone was her madness or dumbness. She became normal. The crowd witnessed these miracles and fell prostrate at the *faqir's* feet and sought His blessings.

Baba's Second Visit to Shirdi

After staying at Dhoopkheda for a few says, the young *faqir* (Baba) accepted the request of Chand Bhai Patil to accompany Him and the marriage party of Chand Bhai's nephew Hamid (son of his younger brother Amin Bhai) who was to be married to Chand Bhai's niece at Shirdi. The marriage party reached Shirdi in bullock carts. The bullock

Sojournings

carts halted outside Shirdi, near Khandoba Temple. When the young *faqir* got down from the bullock cart, Mlahaspati recognised him and addressed him spontaneously with joy, *"Ya Sai"* (Welcome Saint). While the marriage party went to the bride's house, Baba stayed with Mlahaspati for some time. There is a story of how Baba accepted this name 'Sai' given by Mlahaspati. Baba told Mlahaspati that He would accept this new name after a few days. When the marriage was over and Chand Bhai and his party were to return to Dhoop Kheda, he requested Baba to accompany them but Baba told him that He would henceforth stay there at Shirdi.

After a few days, Baba called Mlahaspati and some villagers and asked them to dig the ground under the *neem* tree where He used to stay during His earlier visit to Shirdi — the spot which He used to call *Gurusthan* of the Guru of one of His previous lives. He said, "If after digging the land there, four earthen candles would be found in the ground, I would accept the name 'Sai' forever." This actually happened on digging and so He gladly accepted this name and from that day onwards He was called "Sai Baba" or 'faqir Sai' by all the villagers.

On the day of His arrival at Shirdi, He was dressed in a long, loose white *kurta*, and a green coloured *kafni* (headdress) and over it a *bhagvi* (ochre coloured cap). He had a small *danda* (baton) and a *chilam* (clay pipe) in one hand and He carried the 'brick' in a cloth in the form of a *potli* (bag) hanging on His other shoulder.

Mlahaspati respected Him, but considering Him to be a Muslim did not allow Him to stay in the Khandoba Temple or his own house in the village. For a few days, the father-in-law of Hamid (who was also perhaps named as Amin Bhai of Shirdi) fed Baba while He chose to stay at His old place, the *neem* tree of His *Gurusthan*. Once there were heavy rains which caused a sort of flood. Water and dirt of the village flowed over the body of Sai Baba who was half reclining in the state of *samadhi*. Mlahaspati and other villagers were pained to see Him in such a condition. They persuaded Him not to stay there in the open any longer but to stay in an old, dilapidated, mud-built and long foresaken mosque outside Shirdi, quite close to the *Gurusthan*. Thus, He shifted to the old mosque which He named as 'Dwarka Mai Masjid'.

Ramgir Bua was a boy of 8-9 years of age studying in the village primary school when Baba had come to stay in Dwarka Mai Masjid from 1858 or 1859. In his memoirs of Sri Sai Baba of those days, he writes:

When Baba came (to Shirdi), He had long hair flowing down to His buttocks. He wore a green skull cap over his hair and over it a *bhagawi* (ochre coloured) *topi* with a *chilam* and matchbox.... He got his bread by begging. Yamunabai's mother-in-law (Teli Narayan's wife), next door to the mosque used to give him a *roti*.

Tatya Baba Kote informs us that before coming to stay in the *masjid,* village children used to pelt stones at Baba thinking Him to be a mad *faqir* since He used to live for some time in the jungle of thorny *babul* trees near *Gurusthan*.

Shama, who was the school teacher in the Government Primary School, which adjoined the Dwarka Mai Masjid, recalls:

I was an Assistant Teacher in a school which was located in the place where Baba's horse is now stabled. A window of that always looked on to the adjoining mosque. Through that I occasionally watched Baba who was taken by people to be a mad *faqir*. I had no regard for Him then.... I used to sleep in the school. Baba was the sole occupant of the mosque, yet I could hear English, Hindi and many other languages being spoken in the mosque (at night) evidently by Baba. I inferred that he had remarkable powers and began to have faith in Him.

It appears that because of this, Baba one day went to the nearby village of Rahata, met Khushal Chand Sait (Seth) there who suggested to Him to stay in one of the mosques in Rahata permanently. But after a few days of stay at Rahata, during which Kushal Chand served Him with love and reverence, Baba decided to return to Shirdi and stay in Dwarka Mai Masjid permanently.

He used to beg for food two, three times and on some days, even more. He used to beg at the houses of only five persons. Gradually, the villagers of Shirdi developed love and reverence for Him as He started acting as a village *hakim* (physician) who used to give very unconventional medicines as a cure for diseases.

Baba started curing those who cared to ask Him for any miraculous and immediate cure of their physical ailments. He would give crushed leaves, mostly of *Surajmukhi* or anything He could lay His hands on to the patients and these cured wonderfully. Sometimes He used to prepare a *kadha* (boiled mixture) of *sonamukhi* and some other indigenous medicines and gave one cup full of it to everyone present in His *Masjid* once a month for good health. Sai Sharananand has mentioned:

Sojournings

At the start, Sai Baba prescribed and gave medicines but never charged any money for the same. Not only that, but if He found that there was none to look after or nurse His patient, He would Himself be his nurse and serve him. Once it so happened that His patient failed to observe the rules of diet, etc., that He had prescribed and as a result thereof he died. Since that day Baba gave up administering medicines and gave only His *udi* (holy ash) for relief.

About the patient who died, we learn from his cousin, Raghuji Ganapati Shinde Patel:

As soon as Baba came to Shirdi, one Amin Bhai, a Moslem, gave Him food. That Amin Bhai was visiting my *mausi's* (mother's sister) house occasionally. Her son, Ganapati Hari Kanade, aged 35, had leprosy and fever. Amin Bhai told her that a holy man had come to his house and that He could treat her son. Then Baba came in and saw the patient and told Ganapati to catch a cobra courageously as the cobra would not bite a leper. Ganapati caught a cobra and out of its poison, the medicine was prepared and given to Ganapati. He began to improve in a few days, but he did not observe Baba's injunctions to avoid sexual pleasures, so Baba stopped giving him further treatment. The disease developed and Ganapati died.

Although Baba gave up practising as a *hakim* after this incident, He did give *udi* and also other things like groundnuts, grams, sweets, etc., to his devoted patients throughout His life. It may be mentioned that at that time in Shirdi there lived a *vaidya* (local doctor) who was alarmed by Baba's curing the villagers with His free and instantly effective unconventional cures, and fearing that his reputation and income as a *vaidya* would go down for many years, he would constantly oppose Baba and instigate the villagers against Him.

Events from 1858 to 1891

From 1858 to 1891, i.e., for 33 years till Baba turned 53, His name and fame was, by and large, confined to Shirdi and the nearby villages of Rahata and Nimgaon; very few devotees from other places came to Him. There might have been many events in those years, but there are no documentary evidences now available about them. The notable incidents during this period of 33 years were:

i) Baba established *dhooni* (fireplace) in His Dwarka Mai Masjid around 1858 by lighting the wood with the flame of the sacred lamp of His *Gurusthan* or maybe, by miraculous materialisation of fire.

ii) Baba's *masjid* was rennovated by His ardent devotees like Mlahaspati and others and the practice of plastering it with cowdung and decorating it started.

iii) Baba developed asthma around the age of 45 and in 1885 had an acute attack. Baba left His physical body for three days entrusting it to the care of Mlahaspati. The villagers and government officials started seriously thinking of disposing of the dead body after two days but Mlahaspati resisted their efforts saying that Baba's life would indeed return to the body after 72 hours and this actually happened. Baba revealed that He had done this to save the life of Tatya, the son of Bayjabai who had been feeding Him right from the days of His first visit to Shirdi in 1854. Tatya was extremely intimate with Baba and called Him (maternal uncle); Baba had revealed to Bayjabai in 1854 itself that she had been His sister in many of His previous births.

iv) One Muslim magician and wrestler, Moinuddin, challenged Baba (who also sometimes did wrestling with some of the villagers) to a wrestling bout. Baba accepted the challenge, but was defeated. Thereafter, He started covering His head with *kafni*, moved to the nearby jungle for some months and returned to the *masjid* afterwards.

v) In 1890, one elderly Muslim saint, Javar Ali, came to Shirdi; he stayed with Baba and started treating Baba as his disciple. He forced Baba to accompany him to Rahata; they stayed there in a mosque for some weeks; the villagers of Shirdi led by Mlahaspati went in deputation to Him and forced Him by their requests to return to Shirdi. Then as Javar Ali was humiliated by Saint Jankidas in spiritual contest, he fled away from Shirdi leaving Baba at Dwarka Mai.

Events from 1891 to 1918

The name and fame of Sai Baba spread like wildfire in the nearby villages and then to the neighbouring states or regions soon after 1892 when He performed the miracle of lighting the lamps of Dwarka Mai Masjid with water, after shopkeepers refused to give Him oil on Diwali day.

From 1896, Baba started the annual *Ram Navami-Urs Utasava* (celebrations) in order to forge Hindu-Muslim unity in Shirdi and infuse human values and spirituality among all people who participated in these celebrations.

During 1892-1918, He performed many astounding miracles. Many saints and their disciples came to Shirdi to receive Baba's blessings, and countless people of all religions, castes and social standing came to seek Baba's grace, protection and miraculous cures and spiritual enlightenment. The most widely talked about miracles were : Jmaner incident in 1904 in which Baba materialised the horse carriage with its horse, driver and attendant (to carry Ramgir Bua) which had been sent by Baba to deliver His *udi* and *arti* to relieve Mina Tai, daughter of Nana Saheb Chadorkar, who was having a difficult delivery; saving the villagers of Shirdi from plague in 1910; and Baba's assumption of the form of the three-headed divine child Dattatreya on the Dattatreya Jayanti in 1911.

> *I eat in the form of an ant. I eat in the form of a fly that eats. I take what form I choose and eat in that form.*
>
> — **Sri Shirdi Sai Baba**

6

Charismatic Personality

SRI Shirdi Sai Sansthan brought out a beautiful collection of rare photos and pictures of Sri Shirdi Sai Baba in their official journal *Sai Leela* on the occasion of the First Conference of Sai Devotees at Bombay on 1 February, 1992. Their other publications relating to Baba, *Sri Shirdi Sai Sat Charita, Sai Leela* and *Children's Sai Baba,* contain a number of beautiful pictures of Baba. A big lifelike oil painting of Baba done by Shama Rao Jaykar, painter of Ville Parle, Bombay, at the request of Rao Bahadur M.V. Pradhan, after seeking Baba's permission and then having "a good look at Him" in 1916, is now kept in Dwarka Mai Masjid behind the big triangular black stone on which sometimes Baba used to sit in His characteristic posture — placing right foot over the left ankle and touching that foot with His left hand. A beautiful statue of Baba in this characteristic posture in marble stone, sculptured by a famous sculptor, Talim of Bombay, is installed in the Baba's Samadhi Mandir at Shirdi. Such statues of Baba are to be seen in all Sai temples in India and abroad. Besides these, a most unique lifesize statue of Sri Shirdi Sai Baba in His standing posture installed in the Khandoba Temple on the right side, opposite the lifelike statue of Baba's most intimate and ardent devotee Mlahaspati, is of special interest to all those who are eager to see how Baba really looked in His physical body.

Baba's statue in the Khandoba Temple, according to Mlahaspati's son who had also seen Baba during his lifetime, reveals that Baba was a well built man of five feet six inches. He was neither thin nor fat, but well built. One special feature of His body was that He had very long arms

Charismatic Personality

which touched his knees and also long fingers. Shivamma Thayee, who saw Baba for the first time in 1906 and then subsequently met Him a number of times between 1907 and 1917, has recalled in her memoirs:

> He (Baba) had very long hands. The fingers of His hand stretched below His knees. He was having the *Raj-lakshans* (attributes of a majestic ruler). His colour was very fair. He had a sharp nose with big nostrils. He was neither fat nor thin. His eyes were not black; they were blue and deep. Baba's eyes glittered in night like the eyes of a cat or a tiger. I was very much fascinated by the charm of my charismatic divine *Guru*.

Professor G. G. Narke, another contemporary devotee of Baba, in his testimony stated:

> The first impression I got of Sai Baba was from His eyes. They pierced me through and through. Baba was *askhalita brahmachari* (perfect celibate) and His glittering eyes spoke it.

Mrs. Manager, yet another contemporary devotee, has left behind this thrilling graphic portrait of Baba:

> It is very difficult to describe Sai Baba and our experience of Him, but one may talk about some things related to Him.... One's first impression of Sai Baba was derived from His eyes. There was such a power of penetration in His glance that none could continue to look at His eyes. One felt that Sai Baba was reading him or her through and through. Soon one lowered one's eyes and bowed down. One felt that He was not only in one's heart, but in every atom of one's body. Baba's personality has to be understood in this perspective.

Baba put on white tattered clothes. In the early days, He wore a white *kafni* (turban or cloth covering the head) and a shirt. Later on, He started wearing a long *angarkha* (like a dress and loin cloth). He used to wear a *langoti* as underwear inside the *dhoti* (loin cloth) but no *baniyan* (vest). He tied a cloth around his head which was twisted and hung behind His left ear which He did not wash for many days. In early days, Baba used to visit the *takia*, the village resting place for the Muslim visitors, and there He used to sing and dance with small *ghunghrus* (belled anklets) on his feet. He used to sing Persian, Arabic and Hindustani songs of Kabir till 1890.

Baba put on a white coarse cloth dress — a long *kurta* or *kafni* and while taking bath, He used to wear a *langoti* (loin cloth). He did not take bath daily. Sometimes, He did not take bath for 5-6 weeks. Baba used to get Himself shaved by Bala barber, and paid him whatever coins came out of His pocket when He thrust His hand in it. Mostly Abdul used to wash Baba's clothes; after washing His *kafni* it was dried up by placing it on the *dhuni* in the *Masjid*.

By 1912, when Sharananandji first met Baba, some of the teeth of Baba were missing. In her memoirs, Chandrabai Birker has mentioned that Baba had given her one of His teeth: "I have also this tabij enclosing Baba's tooth, which He gave me as a momento." She had gone to meet Him in 1898.

While going out for begging, He carried a cloth on His shoulders, in which He used to keep the bread given to Him in alms. Although a number of pairs of Baba's *Charan Padukas* (leather sandals) are now displayed among the sacred articles once possessed by Baba in the Samadhi Mandir, it is said that Baba did not wear sandals or shoes while walking.

Baba once said to a devotee:

Nana, the only things that can be called Mine are a rag, a *langoti*, a *kafni* (toga), a potsherd, and a (tin) tumbler. See how inexcusably people trouble Me, pester Me and coerce Me. What should be said of this?

Baba's Habits

Many interesting things are now known about Baba's habits. He very carefully and delicately washed His hands and feet before lunch. He took His bath, mostly at the well located in Lendi Bagh, then a somewhat far off jungle. He did not clean His teeth with any twig, brush, powder, toothpaste or salt. He was fond of smoking His *chilum* and although many of His devotees presented him a number of such *chilums,* He just stored them but used His own old *chilum*. Many of these *chilums* are still preserved in the Sri Shirdi Sai Sansthan. Baba also used to allow His devotees to share His *chilum*.

Baba sometimes used to stitch His tattered clothes with needle and thread in the mosque when alone. In the early years, one devotee, Balaji Shimpi, used to give a pair of dress to Baba once a year, but later on he developed an ego so His economic condition fast deteriorated because of it. Baba did not accept any money for His medical cures but He Himself asked for *dakshina* (cash offerings) of modest amounts, like one rupee or even less to anything up to Rs. 200/- or even more, at a time, repeatedly from His favourite devotees and visitors on whom He wanted to shower His grace, or whom He wanted to protect by teaching a lesson of ego-destruction.

Charismatic Personality

Baba used to abuse and even sometimes beat His devotees in anger. It has been said that actually His abuses were really directed towards the evil forces, obstacles, diseases or misfortunes of the devotees concerned, not towards the people as such. Mama Dube, a contemporary devotee of Baba, recalled this experience in 1912:

> ...I went to the gate of the mosque. Baba was in a towering passion, fuming and fretting with a stone in His hand and was moving up and down the mosque. He saw me standing at the gate. In ten minutes, time, He calmed down and took His seat on the *gadi*. That was the place where He should be approached and I went and prostrated. Of his own accord, He said, Take *udi* and go away.

Lakshman Bhatt Joshi of Shirdi recalled:

> As I was quite a boy when I was with Sai Baba, my thoughts were not serious and I cannot repeat the talks He gave. I would run about doing miscellaneous work at the mosque and odd jobs for Radhakrishna Ayi. Madhava Fasli did the same. We would sleep with Baba in the Chawdi. We were allowed to be with Him when none else were allowed. "Bhai, carry that log of fuel here. Bhai, bring that tub of water, etc.", Baba would tell us. I would be feasted on the perpetual flow of edibles that would be presented to and distributed by Baba. He would have basketful of fruits often and we would occasionally purloin some. Baba would sometimes see us and humorously say, "Do not take too much". Often He would abuse me. Once or twice He beat me with His hands. He would occasionally send for me at night, at Chawdi, and ask me to sing, "Sing Ganu's songs or *tukaras*. I would joke by singing songs in His praise lightheartedly. *'Rahama Najar karo ab more Sai'*, etc. Baba would occasionally Himself get into elated spirits and then (when no one else was present) at dead of the night would sing songs Himself, sometimes Kabir's songs, etc. I do not remember anything now of what He sang.

Baba's Lifestyle

Daily Routine

Baba got up very early and sat by His *dhuni* (fireplace). After He finished answering nature's call, He sat quietly for a while. In the meanwhile, Bhagoji Scinde, a leper, came there and undoing the bandages wound around Baba's right hand massaged the hands and the whole body. Then he prepared the *chilum* and gave it to Sai Baba who smoked it, and gave it to Bhagoji for smoking. After the *chilum* had passed hand to hand five or six times, Bhagoji left.

Then Baba got up to wash His mouth and face. He poured a lot of water on hands, feet, mouth, ears and cleaned all parts of His body in a delicate manner. He followed the same process while taking His bath. After washing His mouth, He went out for *bhiksha* (begging alms) to the five fixed places. He would stand in front of the houses of the following blessed persons, begging for alms, in these words:

i) Nandu Ram Marwadi's house:

"*Hey Nandu Ram, bhakari de.*" (O, Nandu Ram, give Me bread.)

ii) Tatya Patil Kote's house:

"*Hey Bayja maa, jevan aan.*" (O, Bayja mother, bring me meals.)

iii) Apaji Kote Patil's house:

"*Hey Appa, bhakari de.*" (O Apa, give Me bread.)

iv) Vamanrao Gondkar's House:

"*Vamanrao, bhakari aan.*" (Vaman, bring Me bread.)

v) Sukh Ram Patel Shelke's House:

"*Sukh Ram, roti de.*" (Sukh Ram, give Me bread.)

Whatever food was offered to Him, He would keep the bread and dry foods in the fold of the cloth hanging over His shoulder, and all liquid foods like *dal*, vegetable soups, curds, etc., He received in a tin pot (*tamrol*) held in His hand. He brought the food to the mosque, put all of it in the earthen plate, mixed it and kept it in the open. Birds, squirrels and dogs took a part of it freely; Baba took some of it and the rest of it was distributed to the devotees. Many devotees brought *thalis* full of various kinds of delicacies as well as simple food like *roti, rice, khichri, pulao*, etc., for Him, but He merely touched and returned them as His *prashad* (consecrated food), accepting only part of it sometimes, most of which He distributed then and there to the devotees present. One bread was daily sent by Him as *prashad* to Radha Krishna Ayi, His great devotee.

After this '*chotta hazri*' (early light breakfast), Baba held a *darbar* (audience) at which most of His devotees and visitors assembled. Baba gave them advice through direct words of instruction, admonitions or through stories and parables. At times, Baba purchased fruits and distributed them among those present, serving some of them with His own hands.

After this *durbar*, Baba went to Landi, a nearby garden. There He stayed for about an hour. After returning from Landi, Baba stayed in the

Charismatic Personality

masjid till 2 p.m. during which interval He allowed Himself to be worshipped by His devotees through individual *pujas* and then a general or common *aarti*.

Then He had His lunch. At that time, a cloth curtain was drawn in the *masjid* and Baba sat behind it and ate. No one was allowed to enter the mosque at that time, or to peep behind the curtain. Again Baba went to Lendi after about three-quarters of an hour. Then He came to the *masjid* and sat there till sunset when He went out for some time and was again seated in the *masjid*. As a rule, there were three general or common sittings or *durbar* during the day — the first one in the morning after breakfast, the second after Baba's return from Lendi, and the third at about 5 p.m.

Baba's contemporary devotees and close workers, like Abdul, have left behind valuable bits of information about Baba's daily routine and habits. Abdul recalls:

> Baba sat behind what is now a pillar-like structure at the Lendi in which a 'Nanda Deepam' or perpetually burning lamp is kept. I generally found that Baba sat behind the Lendi pillar which enclosed the lamp and not in front. From there the lamp was not visible to Him. I never saw Him gazing at the lamp.... I used to fill two pots with water and place them near Baba at the Lendi lamp place. He would sit near two such potfull of water, and He would go on pouring water in various directions. What that was for and whether He would utter any *mantra* while doing so, I cannot say. Other than me, no one else was present when He poured out water as stated above.

Mrs. Manager recalls:

> He would sit in the mornings near His *dhuni* (fire) and wave His arms and fingers about, making gestures which conveyed no meaning to us, saying, *"Haq"*, i.e., God. Purity, strength, regularity and self-denial one always noticed about Him. He would always beg His food. Even during His illness, He never lay bedridden but would get up and go around to beg His food.

Raghuvir B. Purandhare recalls:

> Baba used to be near the *dhuni*, early morning facing south, leaning on a post and doing something. I cannot say what. People were not allowed to go near, not even 50 feet. The *sevakar* could carry on their usual service or work of clearing or replenishing *dhuni,* etc. No one else could go so near as they. He used to utter words like *'Yade Hao.'* They were seldom clear or audible to us at some distance. *'Allah*

Malik, Allah Vali Hai', i.e., God is the Master and Protector, He used to say often and at all times.

Das Ganu Maharaj testifies:

Baba did not say His five *namaz* or even one *namaz*, as Muslims do. When *fatia* had to be done he generally ordered it to be pronounced by someone present. Sometimes He uttered *fatia*. He occasionally used to repeat parts of the *Quran*.

Abdul Rahim Samsuddin Rangari recalls his visit to Baba in 1913:

I found Baba was smeared with *sandal* paste over His hand, face, etc. Moslems do not smear themselves like this. I asked Him how He put on all this. Baba said *"Jaisa desh, taisa vesh"*. (Do as the Romans do). Instead of worshipping their Gods, they worship me as their God. Why should I object and displease them? I am Myself a devotee of God.

Bayyaji Apaji Patel recalls:

I knew Baba since my boyhood. My house was one of the few houses from which Baba took His *bhiksha*, i.e., begged for His bread from the beginning of His life here and upto the end. For some 3 years, Baba would go about 8 times during the day to our house to beg for His bread. Next, for 3 years He visited us for this purpose four times a day. For 12 years He came to us for bread once a day only. From my 11 years onwards, I used to serve Baba. In 1896, i.e., my 7 years, the *Ram Navmi Urs* celebrations began. It was then that Baba allowed Hindus to offer to do *pooja* to Him and Moslems to read *Quran* before Him at the *masjid*.... When Hindus affixed *sandal* paste to Baba, the latter applied *sandal* marks with the hand (*panja* marks) on the walls of the *masjid* and other Moslems did the same. Baba then applied *sandal* paste to Mlahaspati's forehead and some Moslems and Mlahaspati in turn applied it to Baba's forehead. Baba then allowed *namaz* to go on at the mosque and enjoined silence on all others while *namaz* was going on. Baba Himself recited the *namaz* sometimes and that was only on Saturdays. When *pedas* or other sweets were brought to Baba, He uttered the *Kalama* (which is the same as *Fatwa*) over the sweets and then distributed them to all — Hindus and Muslims alike.

Bapu Rao N. Chandorkar states:

All mantras that Baba spoke or recited were Arabic or Persian, and not Sanskrit, so far as I know. Kondaji and Baba recited *fatwas*.

When *'sera'* was brought by people for placing it on the *niche (Kaaba)*, Baba and Kondaji placed it repeating something in Arabic, Persian or some such language.

Chinna Krishna Raja Saheb Bahadur testified as under:

Baba really cared nothing for money or for presents. What He really wanted was deep love...

Prof. Narke found that:

He kept women at a distance. During the day, a very few women were allowed to massage His legs — and that only up to the knee. He was always properly clad and never indecently exposed Himself.

According to Mrs. Manager:

He was always in the all-knowing state. Sai Baba was one whom some people would not understand at all. He would talk to a hawker about some cloth brought for making *kafnis*, higgle-haggle like the most inveterate shopper at a bazaar and bring down the price of the cloth, say from 8 annas a yard to 5 annas a yard and take, say 40 yards. By this act the hasty onlooker would conclude that Sai Baba was being parsimonious or at any rate attached to wealth. A little later, He (Sai Baba) would pay the hawker, sometimes even four times the price settled. Again the hasty onlooker would conclude that Baba was crazy, touched in the brain, or needlessly ostentatious in His misplaced charity. In both cases, the hasty judgements would be wide off the mark and the real reasons for Sai Baba's conduct would remain a mystery to all except those whom He meant to enlighten.

Baba demanded *dakshina* (cash offerings) from many of His devotees and visitors and during the last ten years of His life. He was getting a daily income of Rs. 500 to Rs. 1 000 per day which was more than the salary of a British Governor, but He distributed all His daily income from *dakshina* everyday in the evening to His close devotees and *faqirs*.

In this connection, the following testimonies are pertinent:

i) Chakranaryana, Police Fauzdar at Kopargaon in October, 1918, recalls:

Whatever He got, He scattered with a liberal hand. When He died, we took possession of His cash; that was only Rs. 16/-, and yet daily He was paying or giving away hundreds of rupees. Often we noticed that His receipts were smaller than His disbursements. Wherefrom came the excess for Him to disburse or pay, we could not make out.

This made me conclude that He had divine powers.

ii) Das Ganu reports:

> Several of those that He was regularly paying everyday were subjected to income tax. After Lokamanya Tilak visited Baba (1915-1917), the Income Tax Department directed its attention to the Shirdi Samsthan. Some officer came to Shirdi and watched the income. They first wanted to tax Sai Baba, but (perhaps seeing that He had little left with Him to proceed upon) they taxed His regular donors, viz., Tatya Patel, Bade Baba, Bagua and Bayyaji Patel.

In his renowned Gujarati edition of *Sri Sai Baba* (1981), Baba's eminent devotee Sai Sharananand has recorded that Baba used to pay the following amounts in charity daily to the following devotees:

Bade Baba: Rs. 30-55/-	Tatya Patil: Rs. 15-25/-
Choti Ammi: Rs. 2/-	Jamil: Rs. 6/-
Dada Kelkar: Rs. 5/-	Bhagi: Rs. 2/-
Sundari: Rs. 2/-	Bayyaji Patel: Rs. 4/-
Laxmibai: Rs. 4/-	Other *fakirs* and poor persons: Rs. 8/-

It should be recalled that at that time only one rupee silver coins were in circulation, and that one rupee of that period was equal to more than Rs. 100/- of today.

Abdulla Jan, a young Muslim *faqir* who came to Shirdi from Peshawar side (North-Western Frontier of the undivided India), during Baba's lifetime has left behind these impressions:

> He fed me and other *fakirs* abundantly and I resolved to stay on and lead an easy life at Shirdi with Him. This was in 1913.... Baba was surrounded by crowds in His lifetime and it was hard to find room in the mosque on account of these crowds. What a number of dogs used to swarm round Him whereas now there are very few men and hardly any dogs to be seen at the mosque which is (reported in 1936) as a rule deserted. If Baba's splendour was so short-lived and it faded away so quickly, what of me, a poor gnat?

For some years till 1910, on certain days, most probably on Thursdays, Baba used to cook *pulao* rice or sweet rice or some other delicacy in the big *handi* (pot) in the Dwarka Mai Masjid. There are some very thrilling accounts of the eyewitnesses. Some of these from *Shri Sai Sat Charita* are

Charismatic Personality

reproduced hereafter.

"...When He took it into His mind to distribute food to everyone, He made all preparations Himself from the beginning to end. He depended on nobody and troubled none in this matter. First, He went to the bazar and bought all the things, corn, flour, spices, etc., for cash. He also did the grinding. In the open courtyard of the *Masjid,* He arranged a big hearth, and lighting a fire underneath kept a *handi* over it with a proper measure of water. There were two kinds of *handis,* one small and the other big. The former provided food for 50 persons, the latter for 100. Sometimes He cooked *mithe chawal* (sweet rice) and at other times *pulao* with meat. At times, in the boiling *varan* (soup) He let in small balls of thick or flat breads of wheat flour. He pounded the spices on a stone-slab and put the thin pulverised spices into the cooking pot. He took great pains to make the dishes very palatable. He prepared *ambil* by boiling *jawari* flour in water and mixing it with buttermilk. With the food, He distributed this *ambil* to all alike. To see whether the food was properly cooked or not, Baba rolled up the sleeves of His *kafni* and put His bare arms in the boiling cauldron without the least fear and churned the whole mass from side to side, and up and down. There was never any mark of burns on His arm, nor fear on His face.

"When the cooking was over, Baba got the pots in the *masjid* and had them duly consecrated by the *moulvi* (Muslim priest). First He sent part of the food as *prashad* to Mlahaspati and Tatya Patil and then He served the remaining contents with His own hands to all the poor and helpless people, to their heart's content.... Those who were accustomed to eating meat were given food from the *handi* as *prashad* and those who were not accustomed were not allowed to touch it.

"...The *handi* business went on for some time till 1910 and stopped thereafter... Das Ganu spread the fame of Baba by His *kirtans* far and wide in Bombay Presidency ...people began to flock to Shirdi and devotees brought with them various articles for presentation and offered various dishes as *naivaidhya* (offerings). The quantity of *naivaidhya* offered by them was so much that the *fakirs* and paupers could feed themselves to their heart's content and there would still be some surplus."

Dhumal, Pradhan and Shivamma Thayee had witnessed Baba cooking food in the *handi* at the Dwarka Mai Masjid and they have corroborated the above description in their testimonies. On her first visit, with her husband, her one-year-old son and lady servant, to Shirdi in 1908, Shivamma Thayee witnessed the Baba's *handi* scene:

Baba was fond of cooking for His devotees. On my first visit to Shirdi I myself saw Him preparing *ragi* gruel in a big pot in the Dwarka Mai Masjid. Wood was burning in the *chullah* and the *ragi* gruel was boiling. Baba pulled up His sleeve and immersed His right hand in the boiling contents of the cooking pot and stirred it many times. We were surprised to see this great miracle of Baba. Evidently, there was no affect of the boiling contents on His hands. Many people besides me and my family witnessed this sort of cooking done by Baba with rapt attention and wonder, repeating Baba's name silently in our hearts. When the cooking was over, Baba Himself distributed the food, His *prashad*, to all devotees, and even to animals and birds who happened to come to the *masjid* at that time.

Prof. Narke has recalled that in 1914, one day Baba got a number of *kafnis* prepared and distributed them among His devotees in the presence of Narke, refusing to give one to him saying, "Do not blame Me for not giving you a *kafni*. That *fakir* (God) has not permitted Me to give you one."

Baba's Behaviour towards His Devotees

Baba treated His devotees with love and concern. He protected them from their misfortunes through His miracles and words of advice. The devotees worshipped Him as God. They loved Him but at the same time were very much afraid of Him. It was customary for devotees to seek His permission before leaving Shirdi, otherwise they suffered many inconveniences or even misfortunes on the return journey. Usually Baba would ask the devotees to wait for a few days or at least for the next day.

Rao Bahadur Dhumal racalls:

When I craved for leave, Baba said in His characteristic fashion (reminding one of the forms of regal veto) "...The King will consider..., i.e., We shall see (what to do) tomorrow. He stopped Me (at Shirdi) for three days."

Baba used to bless His devotees and departing visitors by placing His hand on their heads and pressing it. Sanyasi Narayan Asram informs us:

Baba had a way of touching (with His palm) the head of the devotee who went to Him ...His touch did convey certain impulses, forces, ideas, etc. Sometimes, He pressed His hand heavily on the head as though He was crushing out some of the lower impulses of the devotee. Sometimes, He tapped, sometimes He made a pass with the palm over the head, etc. Each had its own effect — making remarkable difference in the sensations or feelings of the devotee.

Devotees had started the practice of washing His feet and taking the *pada-tirtha* (holy water) at the time of seeking Baba's permission for their departure from Shirdi. W. Pradhan has recalled how Babu Chandorkar had placed a plate under Baba's feet and pouring water on them collected the water to be used at home. "That was a departure in the traditions of Shirdi. Till then only *udi* was allowed to be taken away and *pada-tirtha* was immediately used up at the *aarthi* or at any rate at Shirdi itself. I too took a cue from Babu and carried Baba's *pada-tirtha* home for the use of my mother and others."

Prof. Narke reveals that Baba was living in and operating other worlds also besides this and in an invisible body:

Baba was frequently talking of His travels in an invisible body across distances of space (and time).... In the mornings, sitting near His *dhuni* (fire) with several devotees, He would say to what distant places He went overnight and what He had done. Those who had slept by His side at the *masjid* or *chavadi* knew that His physical body was at Shirdi all the night. But His statements were literally true and were occasionally verified and found correct. He had travelled to distant places in an invisible, i.e., spirit form, and rendered help there. Again, He would frequently talk of *post-mortem experiences.*

A Shirdi Marwadi's boy fell ill and died. People returned from the funeral to the *masjid* with gloomy faces. Sai Baba then said of that boy, 'He must be nearing the river now, just crossing it'. I felt that the reference could only be to *Vaitarni* (river in Heaven).

A research into the whole of Sai literature has revealed us that throughout His 80 years of long life, Baba wept only twice — when His ardent devotee Megha died on 19 January, 1912, and when Baba's most cherished possession, the 'brick', had broken as it accidently fell from the hand of the servitor, Madho Fasle one morning in early October 1918.

Khaparde has recorded Megha's death in his *Shirdi Diary* in these poignant words:

Sai Baba came just as the body of Megha was brought out and loudly lamented his death. His voice was so pathetically woeful that it brought tears to every eye. He followed the body up to the bend in the main road near the village and then went His usual way. Megha's body was taken under the *vata* (banyan tree) and consigned to flames there. Sai Baba could be distinctly heard lamenting his death even at that distance and He was seen waving His hand and swaying as if in *Arti* to say goodbye (to the departed soul).

When the brick fell from the boy Madho Fasle's hand while he was cleaning the *masjid*, Baba shed tears, saying:

> It is not the brick that is broken; it is my destiny. It has been my life's companion and I meditated on the self with its help; it is my very life. It has left me today. I shall not survive for long.

Baba's Unconventional Ideas and Unorthodoxy

A deeper probe into the contemporary devotees' experiences enables us to discover that although Baba believed in the sanctity of one's religious beliefs and did not make fun of or condemn the iconoclast like Kabir (His earlier incarnation), yet He demonstrated the hollowness or futility of many traditional beliefs and practices. For example, Das Ganu and Kusha Bhav have recalled how Baba teased them for observing the food taboo of not eating onions which Baba ate relishingly everyday. Baba did not approve of the Hindus fasting to earn spiritual merits or *punya* and devotees' keenness to get a *Gurumantra* from Him. *Shri Sai Sat Charita* records the story of Mrs Radhabai Deshmukh who resorted to fast unto death in order to compel Baba to give her a *mantra*. Baba addressed her in these poignant words:

> Oh Mother, why are you subjecting yourself to unnecessary tortures and hastening your death? You are really my mother and I am your child. Take pity on Me and hear me... I served him (my Guru) long, very long; still he would not blow any *mantra* into my ears... Oh mother, My Guru never taught Me any *mantra*, then how shall I blow any *mantra* in your ears? Do not try to get *mantra* or *updesh* from anybody. Take Me as the sole object of your thoughts and actions and you will, no doubt attain *paramartha*, the spiritual goal of your life.

Baba did not believe in the traditional concepts of pollution. He asked sweets for *naivaidhya* to be bought from a confectioner's house even when the wife of the confectioner had died of plague in Shirdi on that day and her dead body was lying there. He distributed the sweets so bought from there among His devotees without the least worry about physical or cultural pollution.

He did not keep lepers away from Him. Bhagoji, a leper was His close devotee who bandaged the burns on His right arm and massaged His

Charismatic Personality

body daily for many years, and Baba even shared His *chilum* with him. Mrs. Manager recalls another thrilling incident relating to a leper from whom Baba accepted *pedha* (milk sweets) and distributed it among the devotees and ate a part of it Himself as well:

> On one occasion, as I was seated at a short distance from Sai Baba, there came a leper to the mosque. His disease was far advanced. He was stinking and had little strength left in him so that it was with much difficulty and very slowly, he clambered up the three steps of the mosque, moved on to the *dhuni* and I, feeling the stench from him intensely, hoped he would clear off. At last when he got down slowly carrying a small parcel wrapped in a dirty cloth, I felt relief and said unto myself, Thank God, he is off.
>
> Sai Baba at once darted a piercing glance at me, and I knew that He had read my thoughts. Before the leper had gone far, Sai Baba called out and sent someone to fetch him back. The man came. It was again the slow process of his clambering up, emitting foul stench all the time; and as the man bowed to Baba, Baba picked up that parcel, saying "What is this?" and opened it. It contained some *pedas* and Sai Baba took a piece and of all the people present gave it to me only and asked me to eat it. What a horror to eat a thing brought by the stinking leper. But it was Sai Baba's order, and there was no option but to obey. So I ate it up. Sai Baba took another piece and Himself swallowed it and then sent the man away with the remainder. Why he was recalled and I alone became the chosen recipient of His *peda* none then understood but I knew fully well that Sai Baba had read my heart and was teaching me a valuable lesson in humility, fraternity, endurance and trust in His Supreme wisdom rather than in my own notions of hygiene and sanitation for safety from disease.

Baba taught a dowry-hungry person a lesson. He did not differentiate between rich and poor, Hindus, Muslims or others. His *durbar* was open to all. All sorts of people came to Him to show their skills and offer their regards and receive His blessings, charities and protection. The author of *Shri Sai Sat Charita* recalls:

> In the *durbar* of Sri Sai, many personalities appear and play their part, astrologers come and give out their predictions; princes, noblemen, ordinary and poor men, *sanyasis, yogis,* singers and others come for *darshan*. Even a *mahar* comes and making a *johar* (his salutation) says that Sai is the *mai baap* (parent) who will do away with our rounds of births and deaths. So many others, such as

jugglers, *gondhalis*, the blind and the lame, *Nathpanthis*, dancers and other players come and are given suitable reception. Biding his own time, the *Vanjari* also appeared and played the part assigned to him.

Baba's personality had the essential element of humour also. We come across some interesting examples of His humour. Often He would put on the turban of one of His close devotees and mimic the manner of his walking. Once He pinched His devotee Shama's cheeks with love out of humour. Another time, He described His illness in a humorous language to Khaparde. Baba humorously called Abdul by the nickname of 'My *kava* (crow)'. Once Haridwar Bua had a strange experience at Shirdi. Amambhai Chote Khan reported this:

> A sparrow used to sit on His head as He went until He dipped for His bath at the stream at the village border. Then, it would go up and sit on a tree and resume its seat on His head after the bath was over. We saw this. In our presence, Haridwar Bua asked Baba what this phenomenon signified. Baba said, *'La ilaha illilha. Kya bada durbar hai. Munshiji to andha hai. Sardarji chutia hai. Allah Malik hai. Allah achha karega.'* (God is great. What a great *durbar* it is. The Minister is blind, the Chief Minister is a fool. God alone is the Master. He will set things right.)

Once while massaging Baba's body, the faces of an old man and an old lady touched, and the lady humorously complained to Baba that He wanted to kiss her. Baba enjoyed the humour and commented, "What harm is there in kissing one's mother?"

In order to accomplish a grand *avataric* role, He adopted certain distinguishing role-functioning styles of His own, which included the following:

i) *Setting before People His Ideal Life Model*
All the testimonies presented above unmistakably establish that Sai Baba had an impeccable character. He had no attraction for wealth, women, grandeur, publicity or influence. He had no likes and dislikes of His own. He had no enemies, no family, institution or favourites to worry about. He was truly a model of *Brahamajnani,* and His life was a unique demonstration lesson of "Simple Living and High Thinking" and "Secular in Practice" to all learners from diverse socio-cultural and economic backgrounds. He taught mainly through the example of moral and spiritual life that He Himself led. The charm or charisma of His total personality influenced most of the people.

ii) *Using Miracles to cure and guide People*

Sai Baba employed His remarkable powers to read people's mind instantly, to immediately know diverse happenings of the past, present and future, far or near — in every case, to provide miraculous cures, protection and help to most of His devotees and visitors, and to reform people and help them in their spiritual elevation. He had tremendous control over the forces of nature and the destinies of all creatures. He occasionally demonstrated His powers to protect, guide and help His devotees. Although He could do any miracle, it was not in His role-functioning style to do the miracles of materialising *vibhuti, kumkum, haldi, amrit,* honey, *shivlinga,* lockets, rings, watches, ornaments, pictures, medicines, diamonds, etc., and leaving them behind at the devotees houses as His visiting cards as is the role-functioning style of Sri Sathya Sai Baba today. Sri Shirdi Sai Baba did not need to do such miracles of 'Visiting Cards' as most of the illiterate or even less educated people in those days were simple-hearted and pious people having a great deal of faith and veneration for the divinity.

iii) *Baba's Appearance in Devotees' Dreams*

Devotees' Experiences of Sai Baba and other books on Him are full of examples in which Baba appeared in the dreams of many of His devotees to guide, correct, instruct or bless them. This was His most popular role-functioning style as a divine personality, and He continues to do so.

iv) *Baba's Anger*

Baba often showed His anger by abusing some people and also beating sometimes but evidence confirms the popular belief in the devotees that all His anger, abuses, beating, etc., were in fact directed towards the evil spirits, misfortunes, evil planets, or obstacles in the lives of His devotees or earnest visitors. So they had their inner meanings. On the physical plane, however, they were instruments to discipline, socialise, reform or correct people in the same way as a loving mother or a teacher sometimes beats or shows anger towards a naughty child.

v) *Baba's Humour*

Baba's humour was also one of His role-functioning styles which brought him closer to the hearts of His devotees, relieved them of the atmosphere of tension caused by the fear of Baba's towering personality and created moments of joy, which the participants long cherished.

vi) Baba's Emphasis on Religious Coexistence

The testimonies of devotees clearly indicate that Baba's role-functioning style was characterised by a spirit and an earnest effort to live the ideal of religious coexistence — secularism par excellence. He was born a Hindu, brought up by a Muslim *faqir* and a Hindu *Guru* and He allowed both Hindu and Muslim devotees to pray to Him as *Eeswara* or *Allah*, encouraging both sets of religious beliefs and modes of worship in His Mosque to which He gave the Hindu name "Dwarka Mai".

Nowhere in the world, in any age, can one find a parallel of such a thrilling, matchless and genuine example of divine role-playing as a promoter of religious coexistence and of genuine, simple and pure spirituality. There was no artificiality or element of show-worship or deception in it as is the style of many of the modern Gurus, Acharyas and Godly personalities with their politically supporting patrons and followers.

vii) Baba's Role-functioning Style — a Modified Form of Kabir's style

It is interesting to learn from Baba that He Himself was Kabir in one of His previous births. In both these births, as Kabir and as Sai Baba of Shirdi, the role-sets and the concerns of the two *avatars* were essentially the same — to promote *bhakti* (devotion) of the God in the masses, to make them understand the shallowness or hypocrisy of their fundamentalist stands and diehard rituals and to make them honest, pious, egoless and dedicated beings, who preferred not to become *vanprasthis* (forest dwellers) and *sanyasis* seeking spiritual elevation, but who instead stayed in society, performing their wordly duties in a detached manner, serving humanity and yet rising higher and higher in their spiritual search, not through *dhyana* or *yoga* but by their simple acts of piety, kindness and service to all creatures who had full realisation of the fundamental spiritual truth that all of them had the same soul, all felt hungry and thirsty, all suffered pain and misery and therefore all deserved equal respect and help.

Kabir in his role-functioning style was an iconoclast — a ruthless social critic, and a fiery crusading social activist who waged a *jehad* against the Pandits, Mullahs, Mandirs, Masjid, Kaba and Kashi, and all sorts of belief and practices of the Hindus and Muslims, to sterilise their minds of all germs of irrationality, hypocrisy, spiritual blindness and fundamentalism. On the other hand, during His reincarnation in the 19th-20th centuries, Sri Sai Baba chose to play a positive, appreciative, integrative or conjunctive social interactionist role. He allowed the Hindus as well as the Muslims to continue following their own religious and spiritual beliefs and practices, encouraging the reading of Hindu scriptures (*Gita, Vishnu Sahasranama, Yog Vashistha, Jnaneswari,* etc.) as well as the *Quran*. Instead of decrying the *Sakar* gods He demonstrated that they too were as true as the *Nirakar* (formless) God, and that there was only one God and He Himself was that God which was present before all the people at Shirdi.

Thus Sai Baba of Shirdi was in two ways more advanced than Kabir in His role-functioning styles — one, instead of hurting the traditional sentiments, He won the appreciation, love, cooperation, veneration and following of both the communities; and two, He won the gratitude and love of all His devotees and visitors by showering His miraculous blessings in the form of cures, removal of impediments and bestoval of good luck; this Kabir did not do.

What Kabir could not accomplish through hundreds of *sakhis, banis, ramanis,* and *padas* full of spirituality and scathing social criticism, Shirdi Sai Baba accomplished with a very few words of positive and integrative teachings and a few parables and real life stories of the previous births of some creatures. Instead of threatening to shake and demolish their ancient or traditional beliefs, Baba rightly chose to fortify those structures by His love and understanding and then build the edifice of spirituality on them by teaching only the common and most fundamental spiritual truth.

Shirdi Sai Baba's role-functioning style was certainly different from all other previous incarnations of God — many of whom were rulers and warriors born and brought up in royal families who spent many years of their lives fighting with and killing the evil-doers, or those who spent years in meditation in forests and then formed their sects with large followings. Shirdi Sai Baba's role did not envision the destructive role of Shiva; it did not envision the starting of a new sect, cult, religion or a school of spiritual philosophy. He was the *Avatar* of the Kali age who was solely concerned about the promotion of understanding, regard and unity among the followers of all the existing religions and in making everyone conscious that the popular fallacy of the Kali age that "God is dead" was nothing but sacrilegious.

> *I will not allow My devotees to come to harm. I have to take thought for My devotees. And if a devotee is about to fall, I stretch My hands, and thus with four outstretched hands at a time support him. I will not let him fall.*
>
> —Sri Shirdi Sai Baba

7

Devotees

COUNTLESS people came to Shirdi to seek the *darshan* and blessings of Sai Baba during His stay there from 1858 to 1918. It is virtually impossible to discover and recall the names of all those blessed souls. However, two most authoritative publications *Shri Sai Sat Charita* and *Devotees' Experiences of Sri Sai Baba* (in which about 80 contemporary Sai devotees, testimonies have been recorded) mention the names of hundreds of devotees of Sri Shirdi Sai Baba to whom some miracle or notable experience had happened due to the blessings of Baba. Surely, there might be many other people of Shirdi and visitors from outside who were also recipient of Baba's grace, but they have gone unknown and their experiences could not be recorded by early biographers and authors of books on Baba.

Who became Sri Shirdi Sai Baba's Devotees?
One may say that outwardly innumerable people of various places, different religions and castes and varying social and cultural strata became attracted towards Shirdi Sai Baba and so they came to Him. But the reality, as revealed by Baba Himself, was different. According to Him, only the following were coming to Him to become His devotees:

i) Those souls with whom He had close *rinanubandha* (connections) from their several previous births.

ii) Those souls whom He wanted to pull near Him in order to guide, help, transform or liberate.

Devotees

iii) Those souls whom He Himself wanted to come near; none could ever, just on his own, intrude.

The following quotations of Baba clearly substantiate these points:

I draw My man to Me, wherever and however far he might be, like a sparrow with a string tied to its legs.

I will willy-nilly drag anyone who is My man, even if he is in the seventh nether world.

Shri Sai Sat Charita mentions:

One peculiarity of Shirdi pilgrims was that none could leave Shirdi without Baba's permission and if they did, invited untold sufferings; but if one was asked to leave Shirdi, he could stay there no longer. Baba gave certain suggestions or hints when *bhaktas* (devotees) went to bid Him goodbye and to take His leave.

Like a very powerful magnet, Baba pulled towards Him a number of highly blessed souls with whom He had been associated in many previous lives. To the following devotees Baba had clearly revealed that they had been with Him for a number of past births:

Mlahaspati	: Many births.
Shama	: 72 births.
Nana Saheb Chandorkar	: 4 births.
Raghuvira Purandhare	: 7 centuries
Professor G.G. Narke	: 30 births
Hemadpant	: 30 births
Upasani Maharaj	: Thousands of years. Baba told Upasani Maharaj these words of revelation: "There is *rinanubandha* between us. Our families have been closely connected for thousands of years. So we are one."
Mrs. Chandra Bai Borker	: 7 births. Baba said "She is a sister of mine for 7 births."
Boy *Pishya*	: "Pishya was a Rohilla in his previous birth, a very good man who prayed aloud and once came as a guest to

> Sayin Sahib's (Sai Baba's) grandfather. The latter had a sister who used to live separately. Sayin Sahib was a young boy himself then and he playfully suggested that the Rohilla should marry her. Later he did so. The Rohilla lived there with his wife for a long time and ultimately went away with her, nobody knows where. He died and Sayin Sahib put him in the womb of the present mother."

Baba revealed this to Khaparde: He (Sai Baba) told the story of a former birth in which He, Bapu Sahib Jog, Dada Kelkar, Madhavarao Deshpande (Shama), and Dixit were associated and lived in a blind alley. There was His *Murshid* (Guru) there. "He has now brought us together again." Referring to another birth, Baba told, "You were with Me for two or three years, and went into royal service, though there was enough at home to live in comfort."

Baba revealed to Mrs. Lakshmi G. Khaparde about her past lives as under:

> In one of her previous births she was a very fat cow yielding much milk and belonged to a merchant. Thereafter I lost sight of her (for some time) and in the birth which followed she was born to a gardener, then to a Kshatriya and thereafter became the wife of a merchant. Later, she was born in a Brahmin family and one has been sighted after a long time. Let Me partake the food (served by her now) happily with love and give her satisfaction.

This clearly shows that Baba had pulled many of His dear ones of previous births to Him as devotees at Shirdi. The second point that Baba pulled His men towards Him mysteriously is proved by the case studies of Baba's eminently known close devotees like Mlahaspati, Bade Baba (alias Bade *Mian* alias *Fakir* Pir Mohammad Yasin Mian), Chand Bhai Patil, Abdul, Das Ganu, Nana Saheb Chandorkar, Kaka Dixit, Dabholkar 'Hemadpant', Dhumal, Shama, Radha Krishna Ayi, Sai Sharanananda, etc.

Mlahaspati: He was a hereditary goldsmith and the priest of Khandoba Temple of Shirdi. He welcomed Baba and gave the name 'Sai' to Him in 1858 and served and worshipped Him with matchless devotion till Baba's *Maha Nirvana* in 1918. "In fact not only was he the first, in point of time, amongst the worshippers, but he was also the foremost in excellence."

Bade Baba: This Muslim *faqir* who was elder than Baba in age, was the first devotee of Sai Baba. Baba had instructed and helped him at a mosque in Aurangabad for some years during 1854-58, i.e., before Baba came to Shirdi for the second time and settled there permanently. In later years, this *faqir* was pulled by Sai Baba to His Dwarka Mai Masjid in 1909 and he lived with Baba till His *Maha Nirvana* in 1918. Baba used to give him the maximum amount of daily gift (Rs. 30/- to 55/-) out of His daily collection of donations from visitors to Dwarka Mai.

Chand Bhai Patil: He was the rich Nawab of Dhoopkheda village. He was the first devotee of Baba who had witnessed the miracles done by Baba. Baba drew him towards Himself in a mysterious way. In 1858, Baba was seated under a *mango* tree in a forest near the twin villages Sindhon-Bindhon. Chand Bhai, who was searching for his lost mare "Yad" for the past two months, passed that way. Baba attracted him by showing three miracles in no time — showing the whereabouts of the lost mare which was found to be grazing near a stream nearby, materialising a live ember and then materialising water to wet a cloth for clay-pipe. Baba went with him to Shirdi alongwith the marriage party of his nephew.

Abdul: In 1889, Baba appeared in the dream of a Muslim *faqir*, Aminuddin of Nanded, and materialised two mangoes and asked him to give the two mangoes to Abdul, and sent him immediately to serve Him at Shirdi. Abdul served Baba till His *Maha Samadhi*, doing all kinds of services for Sai Baba, like filling water in pitchers, filling oil in lamps, cleaning the Dwarka Mai Masjid and, street in the front of the mosque, washing Baba's clothes, etc., Baba transformed him and told him:

"I have enabled you to cross the river."
"I have turned your clay into gold."

By his dedicated service towards Baba and Baba's constant guidance and training, Abdul emerged as an eminent devotee and a saint.

Das Ganu: (6.1.1868-25.11.1962): Ganpatrao Dattatreya Sahasrabuddhe, a Brahmin of Akolner village, became a sepoy (policeman) in 1891 and later became a Havildar. He took great interest in *tamashas* (village plays) of erotic and sometimes obscene nature and even took part in them. He composed poems, often impromptu. Baba advised him twice to leave police service but he did not pay heed to this advice. Baba created a situation which forced him to resign in 1903 and come to the shelter at Baba's feet. He was implicated in a false misappropriation case, but by Baba's divine intervention was saved. He spent the rest of his life in performing *kirtans* and composing poems and prayers in praise of Sri Shirdi Sai Baba. It was for him that Baba did the well known miracle of materialising the holy water of Ganga from His toes which He sprinkled on his head. However, he did not drink that holy water as he thought that being a Brahmin he would be polluted by drinking the washing of Baba's feet as *tirath* (holy water). Despite his faults and foibles, Das Ganu was one of the notable followers of Baba whose base metal of a petty-minded lewd constable was turned into gold of a saint, who in turn moulded the spiritual destinies of tens of thousands of Sai devotees by his *kirtans*. In his thrilling testimony, he has vividly recalled the miracles, behaviour patterns and teachings of Baba.

Nana Saheb Chandorkar: Narayan Govind Chandorkar, a pious high-caste Hindu, was the Chitnis of the district Collector of Ahmednagar. Baba who knew him from his last four births in which he had been Baba's disciple, sent for him twice but he considered it below his dignity to go to meet a Muslim *faqir* living in an old and dilapidated mosque of a small village like Shirdi. Ultimately, the Collector's order to him to go to Shirdi to make villagers agree to get themselves innoculated and his police subordinate Das Ganu's entreaties to visit Sai Baba of Shirdi to seek His blessings for his barren daughter Maina Tai, impelled Nana Saheb to come to Baba's shelter in 1903. In 1904, Baba did the famous miracle of materialising a horse carriage with its driver and servant to carry Baba's messenger Ramgir Bua (with whom Baba had sent His *udi* and *aarti* to ensure safe delivery of Maina Tai) to the Deputy Collector of Jamner, Nana Saheb Chandorkar. Nana Saheb spent the rest of his life in dedicated devotion and service to Baba. He served Baba's institution, Sri Sai Baba Samsthan, Shirdi, after the *Maha Nirvana* of Baba, for many years till his death. Baba loved him very much and used to have spiritual discussions with him. He watched the promotion of his spiritual and temporal welfare. Many of the great teachings of Baba came to be known to the world only through Nana Saheb. He was the only devotee who was always privileged to sit very close to Sai Baba in the Dwarka Mai Masjid. Narasimhaswamiji has, however, commented that "His (Nana Saheb's) faith in Baba was undoubtedly very great, but still his constitution, or the degree of progress made by him, prevented him from getting lost into Baba."

Kaka Dixit (1864-5.7.1926): Hari Sitaram Dixit, a high caste Nagari Brahmin of Khandwa, did B.A., LL.B. and became a leading solicitor of Bombay. He was the Secretary of the Indian National Congress of 1904 at Bombay. In 1906, on his visit to England he had an accident in London which caused him an injury in the leg which constantly pained. Nana Chandorkar advised him in 1909 to go to Shirdi and seek Sai Baba's blessings. The same year he went to Ahmednagar with some work and was a guest in the house of Sardar Kaka Saheb Mirikar who was a devotee of Sai Baba. Baba had his own mysterious way of bringing Kaka Saheb to Him. Baba's close devotee, Shama, had gone to Ahmednagar to see his ailing mother-in-law; he went to Mirikar's house to meet him; Mirikar gave him a photo of Baba which was reframed for Megha. He asked Shama to take Kaka Saheb to Shirdi to see Sai Baba. Thus he reached the Divine feet of Sai Baba comfortably. Kaka Dixit rendered great service to Baba and His Sansthan by his skill and wisdom. "Dixit offered his *tan* (body), *man* (mind), *dhan* (wealth) at his Guru's (Baba) feet with perfect confidence. He gave up practice as well as society, politics, socialising, etc., which were dear to him in former days, and stuck to Shirdi to render service to Baba and the *bhaktas*, both before and after 1918 up to the very end of his life. He died peacefully, remembering Baba's name on the auspicious *Ekadashi* day on 5 July, 1926, travelling in a Bombay train in the company of Anna Saheb Dabolkar. Baba had appeared in his dream on the previous night.

Hemadpant: Anna Saheb Dabolkar, whom Baba gave the honourable nickname of "Hemadpant" was chosen by Baba to be the blessed biographer of Baba, the author of *Shri Sai Sat Charita*. He was a Brahmin from a poor family. He was a self-made man. Having studied only up to class five and after passing the public service examination, he joined service as a humble village *talati* and rose to the position of *Mamlatdar* and first class Magistrate by the dint of his ability. In 1910, he was drawn to Sai Baba's feet in Shirdi. He was fortunate to receive Baba's permission in 1916 and encouragement to write *Sai Sat Charita* in Marathi which ran into more than a thousand pages; it was later translated into Hindi, English and other languages. After his retirement in 1916, he rendered a great service to Baba and His Sansthan. Baba enabled him to achieve great spiritual advancement by showering His grace on him.

Dhumal: S. B. Dhumal was a leading lawyer of Nasik. He became a devotee of Gajanan Maharaj in 1903 and was drawn to Sri Sai Baba of Shirdi in 1907. Baba's immense blessings were experienced by him in his personal and professional life and spiritual advancement. Baba once told him, "At every step I am taking care of you. If I did not, what would become of you, God alone knows. On another occasion, Baba told him "Bhau, the whole of last night, I had no sleep.... I was thinking and thinking of you all the night." He was instrumental in winning the legal cases of Baba's devotees like Raghu. He was of a great service to Baba and His Sansthan.

Shama: Madhavrao Deshpande alias 'Shama' (the name Baba gave him) was, according to Baba's revelation to him, living in the same lane with the Baba in a former birth. He was a school teacher in the Primary School in Shirdi, a window of which always looked on to the adjoining Dwarka Mai Masjid of Sai Baba. In the beginning, he used to think that Baba was a mad *faqir* and he used to hear voices in English, Hindi, Marathi, Urdu, and many other languages coming from the *masjid* at night. Later on he got attracted towards Baba to such an extent that he left service and was attached to Him wholetime. He was a witness to all His miracles, teachings and actions and He represented Baba in a number of functions and feasts hosted by Baba's devotees. Baba loved him most and was very free with him. His memoirs of Baba throw a great deal of valuable light on His divine life.

Radha Krishna Ayi: She was a Brahmin widow who was deeply devoted to Baba. After her husband's death she migrated from Ahmednagar to her maternal grandfather Advocate Baba Saheb Ganesh's house in Shirdi to spend the rest of her life in devoted service to Sai Baba. She served Baba by cleaning the *masjid* and *chawdi* as well as scavenging the street and serving and providing food to whichever visitor or devotee Baba sent to her house. Her house was considered to be *Shala* (school) for training Baba's devotees, for she was a strict disciplinarian, harsh in speech, yet very spiritual and hard working as well as a hard taskmaster. "She had wonderful powers of thought reading and clairvoyance. When some unusual order came from Baba that such and such a dish was wanted, she would keep it ready and supply it at once.... She was deeply devoted to Sai Baba, and rendered a great service to His Sansthan. Yet it must be admitted that Ayi had a very sharp tongue and many found her incompanionable. But Sai Baba put his devotees there to perhaps develop their power of endurance. Devotee Raghuvir B. Purandhare in his memoirs has recalled about her:

> I spent every minute of my time at Shirdi in service to Sai Baba, in accordance with the directions of Ayi. She made me work hard all day long for Baba mostly at her residence, often at *masjid* and

elsewhere. Radha Krishna Ayi was a personality of a strange sort. She would sing charmingly and with deep emotion. Suddenly, she would break into laughter or melt into tears and either continue slowly with choked voice or stop the song altogether by her sobs.

Another devotee, Chinna Krishna Raja Saheb Bahadur, has given this profile of Radha Krishna Ayi:

Ayi was a noble and affectionate person — an "Ayi" or mother indeed.... She used to get a *roti* (bread) from Baba as *prashad* daily. She lived only for Baba and her delight was to carry out everything that He wanted or was needed for His Sansthan, i.e., institution and devotees. I find that Baba's instructions and help to me came through Ayi, in a peculiar way. Ayi was so open-hearted and kind that from the first day I could confide all my views and plans to her, and she revealed her ideas and plans to me. As for religious progress, she said that we should so act that no other person should guess what we are doing and how we are getting on.

...As for religious exercise, Ayi was an excellent singer with a divinely charming voice and a good knowledge of music. She could play on *sitar*.... She said that many used the name of Vittal, Ram, etc., but that so far as she was concerned, "Sai" was her God and that name was sufficient for her, while I might go on with the Vittal, etc., if I chose.

Ayi died serving Baba wholeheartedly in 1916 and was cremated on the bank of Godavari river about 8 kms from Shirdi.

Sai Sharanananda: Sri Wamanbhai Prangovind Patel, popularly known as Sai Sharananand, was born in 1889 in a small village in Bardoli Taluka of Gujarat State. As a boy of 7-8 years, on a visit to Somnath Temple he saw a *faqir* whom he saw several times afterwards and on his first visit to Shirdi on 11 December, 1911 was surprised to see the same *faqir* in Sai Baba. He passed LL.B. examination in 1912, joined a solicitor's firm, became Principal of Model High School, Ahmedabad, and in 1921 became a managing clerk in a solicitor's firm in Bombay. In 1923, he took *sanyas* and served Sai Sansthan at Shirdi. He was privileged to inaugurate Baba's marble statue in *Samadhi Mandir* at Shirdi in 1952 which had been sculptured by the famous sculptor, Balaji Vasant Talim of Bombay. His book *Sai Sai The Superman* is a remarkable book on Baba. Baba had once revealed that Sharanananda and Balakram Mankad in a previous life resided opposite each other in caves doing penance. In 1913, Baba detained him at Shirdi and asked him to do *Gayatri Purascharan* (continuous recitation of Gayatri Mantra) to wipe off the sins of his past karmas. Baba used to send him to beg food on His behalf and collect donations from visitors and devotees in Shirdi on a number of occasions.

Upasani Maharaj (15.5.1870-24.12.1941): A doyen among Baba's closest devotees was Kashinath Upasani to whom Baba wanted to give all His divine powers and make him a great saint like Him. Baba had revealed to him that he and Baba had been closely associated in innumerable births for thousands of years. He was drawn to Baba on 27 June, 1911. He underwent spiritual training under Sai Baba's strict vigilance. This was a period of fiery ordeal accompanied by fasting, blindness for some time, physical mortification, insult and other forms of austerities. "Sri Sai helped His *Shishya* Kashinath in many ways, to see that he (Kashinath) lost attachment with his body. He showed him the previous *janmas* (births) and the various forms he had inhabited. So he was none of those bodies, and neither the *papa purusha* nor his *punya purusha*, but distinct from them all. Baba told this about him to one Prabhu from Bombay who was jealous of Baba's declaration that He had given everything to the stranger Upasani:

Prabhu : What, Baba, we have been attending upon You for years, and You seem to be conferring a copper plate grant of all Your powers to this stranger, and are we all, therefore, to be neglected? Is it true that You are giving all Your powers?

Baba : Yes, I speak only the truth sitting as I do in this *masjid*. What I have spoken, I have spoken, I have given everything to this person. Whether he be good or bad, he is My own. I am fully responsible for him and as for *sasana* or grant, why a copper grant? I have given him a gold plate grant.

Turning to Kashinath, Baba said, "Think, which is better, copper or gold?

Kashinath : I do not know, Baba.

Baba : See, copper gets corroded and tarnished. Gold does not. Gold remains pure always. You are pure. You are pure *Bhagavan* (God).

However, Upasani Maharaj could not bear the ordeal of Baba's training for long, and left Shirdi one night on 25 July, 1914. He reached Scinde, Nagpur, Kharagpur and delivered discourses. Then he returned to Sakori, a village near Shirdi, and established his famous institution "Kanya Kumari Sansthan, Sakori" for the spiritual regeneration of womenhood.

Mataji Krishna Priya: A resident of Nagpur, she worshipped Shirdi Sai Baba as Krishna and frequently visited Shirdi to seek Baba's blessings. Once she visited Simla. She came to know that Baba had achieved *Maha Nirvana* immediately on 15 October, 1918 at 2.30 p.m. The next day, Shirdi Sai Baba appeared in His resurrected form at her cottage and accepted her hospitality of tea and food, blessed her and left the cottage. Her thrilling story has been revealed by Sri Sathya Sai Baba recently in his discourse on 27 September, 1992. The brief profiles of twelve most prominent devotees of Sri Shirdi Sai Baba who were closest to Him have been presented hereinfore. There were, however, many other well known devotees such as — Chinna Krishna Raja Saheb, Professor G.G. Narke, Sanyasi Narayan Asram, Abdulla Jan, M.V. Pradhan, Rai Bahadur Hari Vinayak Sathe, Damodar Salu Ram Rasane, Ram Chandra Sita Ram Deo, Balwant Kohojkar, Shama Rao Jaykar Painter, Imam Bhai, Chote Khan, Bayyaja Bai, Laxmi Bai, Mrs. Tarkhad, Ram Gir Bua, Tatya, Sagun Meru Naik, K. J. Bhishma, Rajamma alias Shivamma Thayee, etc. These people and innumerable others like them were pulled by Shirdi Sai Baba towards Him through a variety of pretexts and means as their souls had to be given the final liberation push by Him.

Baba's Assurances to His Devotees

Baba had, even in his lifetime, left behind these eleven grand assurances to all future devotees and visitors to His *Samadhi Mandir* at Shirdi:

1. *"Whoever puts his feet on Shirdi soil, his sufferings would come to an end."*

2. *"The wretched and miserable would rise into plenty of joy and happiness, as soon as they climb the steps of My mosque."*

3. *I shall be ever active and vigorous even after leaving this earthly body."*

4. *My tomb shall bless and speak to the needs of My devotees."*

5. *I shall be active and vigorous even from the tomb."*

6. *My mortal remains would speak from the tomb."*

7. *"I am ever living, to help and guide all who come to Me, who surrender to Me and who seek refuge in Me."*

8. *"If you look to Me, I look to you."*

9. *"If you cast your burden to Me, I shall surely bear it."*

10. *"If you seek My advice and help, it shall be given to you at once."*

11. *"There shall be no want in the house of My devotee."*

All these assurances have been found to be materialising by the devotees and visitors to Baba's *Samadhi Mandir* at Shirdi, and therefore the circle of His devotees has been widening more and more during the last seven and a half decades. All sorts of physical, worldly and spiritual problems of the believers in Baba were solved in all cases during His lifetime and they are still being solved.

How far were the Devotees' Motives fulfilled by Baba?

In almost all cases, the devotees' motives or wishes, if they were sincere and full of love and total belief in the mercy of the divinity of Sri Sai Baba, were fulfilled. "I am the slave of My devotees. The faqir in the *masjid* (Dwarka Mai) is so very kind," Baba often used to say. Therefore, whosoever went to Him with deep faith, love, veneration, devotion and decorum found his wish fulfilled, his trouble warded off, his problem solved instantly or within a few days.

Even in most impossible cases which Baba initially seemed to avoid entertaining, if the applicant earnestly prayed and cried, Baba would be moved and wipe out all the bad *karmas* (curses) of fate and save him or her. Four examples are worth mentioning in this connection:

i) Scinde had seven daughters and no son. He went to Dattatreya Temple at Gangapur, 200 miles from Shirdi, and prayed for a son. He got the son within a year, but for six years he did not go to thank the deity there. When he visited Baba at Shirdi, He flared up and told him, "Are you so conceited and stiff-necked? Where was any male progeny in your *prabhakarma* (fate)? I tore up this body (pointing to His own body) and gave you a male child (in answer to your prayer)."

ii) In Damodar Rasane's horoscope, there was the *papi* (sinful or cruel) planet 'Ketu' in the fifth house and astrologers had predicted that he could never have any issue. "But Baba, a *Satpurush*, overcame all that. He anticipated and provided for the issues for so many years. He

Devotees

said 8 children will be born to my younger wife, to whom I was to give the four mangoes that He gave me.

iii) Bhimaji Patil, a critical tuberculosis patient came to Baba. Baba said to him that his disease was due to his very bad evil *karmas* (deeds) and that He was not willing to interfere in it. The patient wept bitterly, caught hold of Baba's feet and prayed to Him for blessings. Thereupon Baba was moved and said, "Do not fear. Your sufferings have come to an end. Whosoever steps into this *masjid* will be relieved of his sufferings, however bad they might be. The *faqir* here is very kind." Soon the spitting of blood stopped and his condition improved. Baba appeared in his two dreams. In the first dream he was flogged by his school teacher for not reciting a poem and in the second dream a heavy roadroller moved up and down his chest causing him intense pain, and in the morning he was completely cured.

iv) Another tuberculosis patient, Mrs. Malan Bai, daughter of D. R. Joshi Devgaonkar, who was after the doctors, lost all hopes of saving her. Baba asked her to lie down wrapped in a blanket and take only water. She followed Baba's instructions carefully but after seven days, one early morning she died. Her relatives were busy making arrangements for her funeral. On that day Baba for the first time did not come out of *chawdi* till 8 a.m. Suddenly she opened her eyes and looked frightened. Baba at the same time came out of the *chawdi*, crying loudly, pouring out wild abuses, striking His staff against the ground and hastened to the place where the girl was lying. The girl recalled that "A dark person was carrying me away; I was very much frightened; I cried for Baba's help. Baba took His staff and beat him, snatched me and carried me to the *chawdi*." She described the inside of the *chawdi* accurately although she had never seen it. This proves that Baba had resurrected her.

Such highly thrilling cases testify to the fact that devotees not merely believed but were hundred per cent assured in their heart of hearts that Baba could and would help them in their hour of crisis.

Mrs. Manager, an ardent contemporary devotee of Shirdi Sai Baba, left behind these empirical impressions of her visits to Him:

It is not merely His power that endeared Him to His devotees but His loving care combined with these powers made Shirdi a veritable paradise to the devotees who went there. Directly we went there, we felt safe that nothing could harm us. When I went and sat in His presence, I always forgot my pain, nay the body itself with all mundane concerns and anxieties.

His accessibility to everyone at all hours was a remarkable feature. "My *durbar* (royal assembly) is always open at all hours." He had nothing to fear from scrutiny, and nothing shameful to conceal. All His actions were open and above board.

Another distinguishing feature of His life was freedom from care and anxiety. He had no interests to serve or protect, no institution to seek support for a maintenance, no acquisition to safeguard, no private property to feel anxious about.

However, in exceptional cases, Baba flatly refused to allow very wicked or sinful persons in His *masjid* and left them on their own to suffer on account of their very bad actions in their past births or past years. Shama Rao Jaykar, who was privileged to seek Baba's permission to do three oil paintings in his lifetime has recalled that Baba spoke these very words before him:

"As you sow, so will you reap."

Prof. G.G. Narke's testimony in this context is very pertinent:

Baba was, of course, adapting Himself to the capacity of people that resorted to Him for help and protection. Most of them were superficial people— seeking mostly some material gain or advantage but when anyone capable of diving deep came to Him, He revealed more of Himself and His powers.... Baba was not the man to stifle legitimate inquiry.

...A saint should not be judged by the character of those that gather around him. Prostitutes, women hunters, avarious people and sinners of various sorts came to Him mostly to gain material advantage, but when they failed to take advantage of His presence to improve themselves, fell into sins and He let them suffer. His justice was severe. 'You have to cut your own child if it falls a threat to the womb' he has said.

What sort of Social Interaction and Mutual Regard existed among the Devotees?

Social interaction processes are of two kinds—integrative or conjunctive social processes, and disintegrative or disjunctive social processes. Integrative processes are accommodation, adjustment, cooperation, integration and assimilation. Disintegrative social processes are competition, conflict, dissension, etc.

A close perusal of literature relating to Sri Shirdi Sai Baba reveals that among the contemporary devotees of Baba there did not exist any undesirable competition, conflict or any other kind of disintegrative tendency, lack of mutual regard or superiority-inferiority complexes, although the devotees came from diverse socio-economic, religious and cultural backgrounds. A great deal of accommodation, adjustment, cooperation and integration was found operative in them and there always was a tendency to respect, help and cooperate with others like brothers and sisters. Baba controlled and guided all of them in this in His direct as well as indirect ways. The fatherhood of Baba as their common living God and the brotherhood of all the children of Baba was the matchless reality of those days. Baba's *Dwarka Mai Masjid* was a unique spiritual university which taught secularism par excellence to Hindus, Muslims and others.

The following portrait of this unique institution of secularism drawn by His contemporary devotee, R. A. Tarkhad, is most revealing:

...When a Mohammedan visitor came to pay his respects with flowers, a lump of sugar and coconuts, *fatia* (Moslem prayers) were uttered in which Baba joined. The flowers were hung in the central niche (of the Dwarka Mai Masjid), the lump of sugar was partly distributed amongst all those present there as well as the village urchins outside and a part of it returned to the party as *prashad*. The coconuts were broken up and similarly distributed. All the while, the Hindu devotees sitting there witnessed this *fatia* and partook the lump of sugar as well as pieces of coconut with pleasure and joy.

The Hindus worshipped Sri Sai Baba with all their rituals as observed in the Hindu Temples. *Sandal* paste was applied to Baba's forehead, chest, hands and feet. *Kumkum* with rice was similarly applied. The toes of His feet were washed and the water partaken as sacred *tirath*. The *aarti* was performed at noon with all the din and paraphernalia of worship as in a temple. Bells were rung. Sacred lamp with its five lights was waved before him, cymbals clashed, the big drum sounded, and a huge bell in the compound sent its notes for miles and miles around and hundreds of devotees recited in perfect union the words of the *aarti* and the sacred Sanskrit hymns. The Mohammedans present there enjoyed all this and freely partook the offerings distributed by the Hindu *bhaktas*.

This wonderful place was called *Dwarka Mai* (by Sri Sai Baba)...in this unique place all the principle creeds were united and the common worship of the universal God brought home to each and all in a unique and loving manner. Moreover, to the ordinary householder, an object lesson for carrying on his daily earthly duties with tolerance for the views and rituals of others was driven home in a most vivid and unmistakable manner.

On the other hand, however, it has been discovered that the fundamentalists among the Muslims of Baba's time did not like His secular and tolerant behaviour. In 1894, Muslims led by a Kazi of Sangamner opposed the worship of Sai Baba in the *masjid* by the Hindus. They went with *lathis* to beat Hindu devotees, but could not do so due to the moral and spiritual courage of Sai Baba. A Muslim Pathan tried to hurt Sai Baba later on. In this regard Abdul's testimony is relevent:

"Besides me, no one else was reading the *Quran* in the *masjid*."

However, we find that besides Abdul some Muslim devotees also read the *Quran* before Baba at diferent times for some days; of course only Abdul read the *Quran* regularly. Fundamentalist Muslims, however, did not do so out of their prejudice. Some fundamentalist Hindus also did not go to Him. Baba did not go to offer *namaz* (Muslim prayer) with other Muslims at any place outside His Dwarka Mai Masjid. During the last decade of Baba's life, these prejudices had weakened considerably and Sai Baba had become the most respected and sought after Prophet by not only the Hindus and Muslims but by the Parsees and Christians as well.

What was the Impact of Baba on the Lives of His Devotees?

Since Baba had, on numerous occasions, demonstrated His control over all the five elements of which all animate and inanimate objects in this universe are composed and He had been blessing and helping all His earnest devotees in their problems of life, His impact on them was very powerful. They had an unflinching faith in Him. They treated Him with utmost veneration, love and regard. Even though He often abused violently and sometimes even beat up some of the devotees, no one took it ill; on the other hand, this was considered to be a blessing — a sure guarantee that the disease or problem of the devotees concerned would soon be over. Baba's words were considered to be the words of *Allah* or *Bhagavan* (God). They conveyed the right message to the concerned person straightaway, whether they were direct words or in the form of parables or stories. People indeed tried to improve their moral character and social dealings as advised by Baba. He became the family deity of all His devotees belonging to different faiths. Many devotees started offering *naivaidhya* (food) to Baba in their homes and to Him directly when in Shirdi. Most of the devotees understood the importance of feeding hungry creatures — dogs, other animals, beggars, destitutes, as Baba had, through innumerable miracles and teachings, convinced them that all creatures have the same soul and one must be full of piety and love towards all creatures. The devotees started realising the futility of religious differences, and genuine emotional integration developed among them. Baba corrected, reformed, transformed and spiritually elevated His devotees. Some of the testimonies of His contemporary devotees very clearly bear this out. Abdulla Jan, a Muslim Pathan originally of Tarbella near Peshawar, wrote these earnest lines:

> ...I was informed (in 1913) when I was at Haripur on the way to Manmad that Sai Baba at Shirdi was a great person who was literally showering money on *faqirs* and would send me to Mecca, if I wanted. So I went to Shirdi.
>
> ...My stay with Baba brought about some changes in my mentality. When I came to Shirdi, I regarded Hindus as enemies of mine. After remaining about three years with Baba, this feeling of animosity passed away and I was viewing Hindus as my brethren. Now, for instance, I see with regret that at Bombay, Hindus wish to destroy Moslems and their mosques and Moslems wish to destroy Hindus and their temples. If both succeed in wiping out each other they will only make room for persons of other faiths to establish themselves in the place of these two.

Did All the Devotees make best use of Baba's Incarnation?
Once a devotee, Damu Anna, asked Sri Shirdi Sai Baba whether all those who came to Him were benefited. To this Baba gave the following reply pointing towards a *mango* tree:

> Look at the *mango* tree in blossom. If all the flowers brought fruit what a splendid crop it would be. But do they? Most fall off (either as flowers or as unripe fruit) by wind, etc. Very few remain.

At another time, He complained to His close devotee, Khaparde, on 7 December, 1911:

> This world is funny. All are My subjects. I look upon you all equally but some become thieves and what can I do for them? People who are

themselves very near to death desire and contrive the death of others. I keep quite. God is very great and has officers every where. They are all powerful. One must be content with the state in which God keeps them. I am (also) very powerful.

Sri Narasimhaswamiji, on the basis of his thorough research into the lives of the close devotees, whom he has called as the "Apostles of Sai Baba", made the comment that the devotees did not make the best use of Baba's contact. He gives the following evidence to prove it:

i) *Shama:* Baba's closest devotee from 1881 till His achieving *Maha Samadhi*, he was so close and informal with Him that he could not realise the fullest spiritual stature of and benefit from Him. Although he received Baba's immense love and spiritual encouragement he did not become a great saint.

ii) *Das Ganu:* Although he was the recipient of Baba's great love and he sang and spread His glory by his *kirtans* throughout the Maharashtra region for years, Das Ganu could not appreciate the importance of the miracle of the flow of Ganga water from Baba's toes due to his orthodoxy as a Brahmin. He has himself admitted:

Theoretically, I knew that he was God Narayan and that Ganges flowed from Narayan's feet but that was a very weak faith insufficient to give my heart the pleasure which a tangible Ganges would give me. Baba knew my mentality and asked me to approach His feet and hold my palm near His feet. The water began to flow from His feet. It was not a few drops like perspiration. It was rather a slow and thin current. In a short time, say a few minutes, I had collected a palmful of that water. Here was the Ganges and I was delighted. I bathed, i.e., sprinkled the water over my head. I did not drink this water. Usually I do not drink the *tirath* offered at Baba's *aarti*....but Baba did not always respect orthodoxy — at least in some matters.

iii) *Khaparde:* In spite of very close contact with Baba not only in His present life but even in the past births and Baba's showering all kinds of protection and love on him and his family and His efforts to raise *satwitkata* in him, Khaparde could not do away with his *rajsik* habit of sleeping in daytime, laziness, sexuality and egoism even at the age of 59. His *Shirdi Diary*, notes Narasimhaswamiji, a most valuable document of Baba's time, hides more about Him than what it reveals about Him and others. "He maintained his old life of thought, that is, great attachment to wealth, comfort, name, position and slight veneer of religiosity combined with respectful life as quite sufficient for his purpose."

...The diary frequently mentions that his position was all in all in his eyes and when others came to Shirdi, he was an institution to be visited by them just as they visited Shirdi. To show him that at the age of 59 he should no longer be thinking of sex gratification, Baba gently gave a hint by calling his wife 'Ajibai' meaning old lady. Khaparde, unable to take the same viewpoint, mentions the same in the diary regarding it as something unintelligible.

iv) *Upasani Maharaj:* Kashi Nath Upasani was groomed as Baba's spiritual heir by Him. Baba showered His greatest grace of spiritual training on him and declared: "Everything I have got I have completely given him." Despite such a rare and most valuable opportunity offered to him, Upasani Maharaj could not make the best use of Baba's contact due to his "older tendencies". Narasimhaswamiji puts it "....what Baba expected was that after four years of novicehood under Him at the Khandoba Temple were over, Upasani would develop into a perfect *Samartha,* a Guru-God for all persons and that Shama would bring Him out from His solitude in Khandoba Temple to a public place so that all may worship Him as the perfect divinity, but this consummation was somehow not to be. It was prevented in various ways. The solitude was repressive and the older tendencies though being snuffed out could not disappear completely".

...In times these contrary tendencies fully developed and wealth (counted in lakhs and taken in the shape of loans, 80 acres of land and hundreds of cattle) was stored up. There was the feeling in Upasani Maharaj and those surrounding him that he was the owner of this wealth which is exactly the view of the Government which levied income tax, etc., on him. The notable point is that as long as he was scattering away wealth as Sai Baba did as soon as it came, till about 1925 or 1926, his popularity was unbounded. He had no enemies.... After 1936, it was difficult to find even a thousand people enthusiastic over Upasani Baba.

These instances show that God's incarnation does not compel even His devotees to change if they do not want to change; God has given everyone 'free will' and he is free to use it as he pleases, God's incarnation only shows him or her the right path and motivates and helps to tread it.

Notwithstanding these, the fact remains that a sizable percentage of Baba's devotees were indeed greatly benefited in their spiritual attainments due to Baba's contact. The cases of Mlahaspati, Abdul, Chandorkar,

Kaka Dixit, Hemadpant, Tatya Saheb Noolkar, Radha Krishna Ayi, Mataji Krishnapriya, Shivamma Thayee, Sai Sharananandji and the like are glaring examples. The life-experiences of Baba's all blessed contemporary devotees teach us to make best use of our remaining days of life as human beings on this planet in accordance with the teachings of morality and spirituality by the great Universal Master, Sri Shirdi Sai Baba.

> *Saints exist to give devotees temporal and spiritual benefits. I have come to give such good things to the devotee.*
> —Sri Shirdi Sai Baba

8

Contemporary Saints

Sri Shirdi Sai Baba as a Unique Saint

The lifespan of Sri Shirdi Sai Baba was from 1838 to 1918. During that long period of 80 years, there were a number of saints in India — some of them were national and even international, while most of them were local saints whose fame was confined to either their own district or state or regional boundaries. A very careful research into the whole of the published literature on Shirdi Sai Baba has revealed to us a number of valuable clues in regard to the origin of Sri Shirdi Sai Baba as a great saint:

i) *As the Chief of Nath Panchayat Ruling the Universe*
Gunaji, English translator of *Shri Sai Sat Charita*, mentioned this:

> It is said that a few centuries ago, there was a *Deshapanchayatan* (group of five sanits) consisting of Samartha Ramdas, Jayaramaswami, Raghunathswami, Keshavaswami and Anandamurthi. Similarly, it is said that there was *Nath-Panchayatan* in those days (during Shirdi Sai Baba's period), consisting of Madhavnath, Sri Sadguru Sainath, Dhundiraj Palusi, Gajanan Maharaj of Shegaon and Gopaldas (Narsing Maharaj) of Nasik and they all worked together by inner control or force. ...Sainath (Baba) had great respect in this *Panchayatan* and was referred to as *Trilokinath* and *Kohinoor* by Madhavnath."

ii) *Sai Baba As a Nathpanthi Saint*
American spiritual philosopher and researcher, Professor Charles S.J. White, has tried to show that Shirdi Sai Baba was actually in the *Nathpanthi* tradition of *Nath Pirs* like Guru Gorakhnath, Kabir and many

others. The characteristic features of *Nathpanthi* saints were: having their *dhuni* (fireplace), Hindu rituals with lights and incense, yogic connections and feats or miracles, love for animals (chiefly dogs), living like *faqirs* and helping the poor by their teachings, miracles, etc. Shirdi Sai Baba had all these features. Kabir in his early career had also come under the influence of Guru Gorakhnath's cult. Shirdi Sai Baba himself revealed in His lifetime that in one of His earlier incarnations He had been Kabir. The view of Gunaji, as stated above, lends further credibility to this view.

The *Nathpanthi jogis* or *yogis* have been having a great deal of interaction with Muslim modes of worship, Muslim saints and cultural traits of Islam, although they have essentially been Hindus. They have been universal and secular in their pattern variables — in their beliefs, ideas, practices and social interactions as well as worldview. They have been having their ears pierced and they have not been circumcised like Muslims. Sai Baba of Shirdi shared all these characteristics of *Nathpanthi Pirs* (saints). Like Gorakhnath who gave his miraculous *bhabhuti* (vibhuti or holy ash) to the ailing and suffering people, Sai Baba also started giving the *udi* (holy ash) of His *dhuni* in Dwarka Mai Masjid right from 1858.

iii) *As Chief of the Five Perfect Masters of the Universe*
According to Sri Mehar Baba, an important *Avatar* of our age:

> These Perfect Ones or God-realised Ones are fifty-six in number in the world at all times and this number includes five Perfect Masters who come out in the open and are ever present. They are always one in consciousness although they are different in function. They are God-personified who control and look after the affairs of the Universe.

Aiyer, author of *Perfect Masters,* adds to this clue by recalling that the *avatars* and Perfect Masters always function in cooperation with a band of saints or workers and their number varies in different incarnations or from saint to saint. For instance, the scriptures tell us that the *Devas* (gods) were born as *vanaras* (monkeys) to assist Lord Rama; *gopis* were actually gods and goddesses who had incarnated to assist Lord Krishna in His divine drama. Jesus Christ also had twelve disciples.

In pursuance of this religious belief and seemingly rational argument, it is quite in order to believe that when Sri Shirdi Sai Baba incarnated as an *avatar,* a whole galaxy of saints had also to take birth and function as saints, as spiritual collaborators or adjuncts of Sri Sai Baba in the divine drama, or in His role-functioning as an *avatar* during the later half of the 19th century and the beginning of the 20th century.

Our curiosity naturally is awakened at this point. Sai Baba was one of the five Perfect Masters; who then were the other four Perfect Masters? Aiyer has not given an answer to it directly, but in his book *Perfect Masters,* he gave profiles of Upasani Baba, Tajuddin Baba, Baba Jan, Narsing Maharaj and Mehar Baba besides that of Sri Shirdi Sai Baba.

Bhardwaj cites a very interesting revelation in this connection:

> One day at 6 a.m. when he (Mankewala) was lying awake in bed, Baba (Sri Shirdi Sai Baba) appeared before him (in 1948) and said, "I am not a *fakir;* I am the *avatar* of Lord Dattatreya. The same Lord is carrying on his divine mission assuming the different forms of Tajuddin Baba of Nagpur, Dhunivale Dada of Khandwa, Sri Visnudevanand Saraswati of Narmada, Sri Swami Samartha of Akkalkot and myself.

iv) *As Avatar of Lord Shiva*

Sri Sathya Sai Baba, who has claimed to be the reincarnation of Sri Shirdi Sai Baba, has stated that Lord Shiva had incarnated as Sri Sai Baba of Shirdi. In this connection, the following extract from B. V. Narasimhaswami, the well known prognostic of Baba's name, is worth serious consideration:

> The Supreme Being is thought of as having five aspects or functions, with names appropriate to each:
>
> | | |
> |---|---|
> | *Creation* | : Brahma in conjunction with Saraswati. |
> | *Maintenance* | : Vishnu or Narayana in conjunction with Lakshmi. |
> | *Destruction* | : Rudra in conjunction with Kali. |
> | *Protection or Ruling* | : Ishwara (Shiva) in conjunction with Maheshwari. |
> | *Redemption* | : Sadashiv in conjunction with Kripa. |

There are *avatars* combining often several of these elements. The life work of a *Samartha Sadguru* (Perfect Master) leads one to identify with the redemption of the Supreme Being.

From these functions, the aspect of Protection or Ruling definitely was the most predominant or the theme feature of Sri Shirdi Sai Baba and, therefore, He was undoubtedly Shiva *avatar.*

It will be racalled that when the *faqir* Patil's wife Faqiri was carrying Baba (child Babu) to Guru Venkusha's *ashram* at Sailu, Venkusha had a dream the previous night in which Lord Shiva had appeared before him and told him that He Himself was coming to his *ashram* at 10 a.m. next morning.

v) *As Avatar of Lord Dattatreya*

Sri Shirdi Sai Baba appeared in the form of three-headed divine child Dattatreya before a group of His devotees on Dattatreya Jayanti in 1911, and Balwant C. Kohjkar had himself witnessed this miraculous revelation. This has been corroborated by his son, Sanker Balwant Kohjkar's testimony.

vi) *As the Supreme One (All Gods and Godesses Rolled into One)*

All the above clues to the reality of Sai Baba are undoubtedly true but truer than all these was what He Himself declared and revealed through His behaviour pattern and actions. He had declared this about Himself:

"I am not confined within this body of 3½ cubits-height; I am everywhere; see Me in every place."

"People think they are all different from each other. But in this, they are wrong. I am inside you. You are inside Me.

"I am the Inner Ruler of all hearts and seated in them."

"I am the Controller - the Wirepuller of the show of this Universe."

"I am omnipresent, occupying land, air, country, world, light and heaven and that I am not limited."

"I am the mother - Origin of all senses, the Creator, Preserver and Destroyer. Nothing will harm who turns his attention towards Me, but *maya* will lash or whip him who forgets Me. All the insects, ants, the visible, movable and immovable world is My Body or Form."

Thus He professed to be the Supreme Being, the Almighty God, who has been and is still being worshipped in numerous forms of gods, goddesses, prophets, saints and masters in different religions throughout the world.

Not only did He profess as such, but He actually demonstrated all this very convincingly with transparent sincerity and honesty before all those who saw Him, lived with Him, visited Him and became His devotees.

Although He was a Brahmin, He never tried to assert this fact. Although He was aware of His parentage and place and circumstances of birth, He did not want to disclose these to the people as He did not want to have any worldly links with His relatives or people of Pathri village. Although He was Himself God incarnate — *Ishwara, Allah* or *Bhagavan* — instead of asserting this fact over and over again, He usually described Himself as *"faqir"* or *"Allah's servant"*. He used to say, *"Allah Malik Hai"* (God is the Master), thus implying that He Himself was merely a servant of God who carried out Allah's or God's orders or wishes.

The following factual portrayal of Sri Shirdi Sai Baba as presented in *Shri Sai Sat Charita* very clearly reveals His true identity as a unique universal saint who had genuine regard and concern for the saints and followers of all religions, and who in turn was the recipient of the adoration, love and worship of the saints and followers of other religions.

Let us see what sort of personage was Sai Baba. He conquered this *sansar* (worldly existence) which is very difficult and hard to cross. Peace or mental calm was His ornament. He was the home of Vaishnav devotees, most liberal (like Karna) amongst liberals, the quintessence of all essences. He had no love for perishable things and was always engrossed in self-realisation. He felt no pleasure in the things of the world or of the world beyond. His *antarang* (heart) was as clear as a mirror and His speech like nectar. The rich and the poor were the same for Him. He did not know or care for honour or dishonour. He was the Lord of all beings. He spoke freely and mixed with all people, saw the acting and dances of nautch - girls and heard *ghazal* songs and still never swerved an inch from *samadhi* (mental equilibrium). The name of *Allah* was always on His lips. While the world awoke, He slept and while the world slept, He was vigilant.

...If you think that He was a Hindu, He looked like a *Yavan* (Muslim). If you think Him to be a *Yavan*, He looked like a pious Hindu. No one definitely knew whether He was a Hindu or a Mohammedan. He celebrated the Hindu festival of *Rama Navami* with all due formalities and at the same time permitted the 'sandal' procession of the Mohammedans.... If you call Him Hindu, He always lived in the *masjid;* if Mohammedan, He always had the *dhuni* (the sacred fire) and other things which are contrary to Mohammedan religion, i.e., grinding on the handmill, blowing of the conch, ringing bells, oblation in fire, *bhajan,* giving of food, and worshipping of Baba's feet by means of *arghya* (water) were always allowed there. If you think that He was Mohammedan, the best of

Brahmins and Agnihotris, leaving aside their orthodox ways, fell prostrate at His feet.... Sai Baba was such a saint who saw no difference between caste and creed and even beings and beings. He took meat and fish with *fakirs,* but did not grumble when dogs touched the dishes with their mouth. ...How could He, who even in dreams never warded off cats and dogs by harsh words and signs, refuse food to poor and helpless people? He saw divinity in all beings. Friends and foes were alike to Him. He even obliged the evil doer and was the same in prosperity and adversity. No doubt ever touched Him.

The Galaxy of Sri Shirdi Sai Baba's Contemporary Saints

Shri Sai Sat Charita has rightly mentioned "There have been institutions of saints in this world from time immemorial. Various saints appear (incarnate) themselves in various places to carry out the missions allotted to them, but though they work in different places, they are as if they were one. They work in unison under the common authority of the Almighty Lord and know full well what each of them is doing in his place and supplement His work where necessary." There were about 54 saints who were the contemporaries of Sri Shirdi Sai Baba and were in contact with Him in some form or the other and about whom some information is available in the literature on Sai Baba. In this regard, the following points are worth consideration:

1. Not only in His life as Sai Baba of Shirdi in the 19th-20th centuries, but even in a number of His previous births He had been a saint. It may be recalled that He was an incarnation of Dattatreya, He was Kabir. He was that saint *(faqir)* who had assured the distressed ruler of India Humayun, that a son would be born to him at Umrakot and he would be the Emperor of the country, and He had met the great Hindu celebate spiritualist of Kashi (who incarnated as Emperor Akbar). He had been leading saintly lives at different times.

2. The very circumstances of His birth and upbringing reveal that all around Him were saints or saintly people. His father Ganga Bavadia had already decided to become a renunciate and had actually left his house. His mother, Devagiriamma, also had decided to become a renunciate and follow her husband to the forest. His father did not even wait for her delivery in the forest and went away in utter *vairagya*, leaving Devagiriamma all alone in the forest where she delivered the child. She also abandoned the child in the forest soon after the birth and went following her renunciate husband's footsteps.

Then, *faqir* Patil and his wife Faqiri found the newborn baby; they took it with them to their house at Manwat and brought Him up. They named the child *Babu*. Thus in His childhood itself Baba was cultivated into *faqiri* (mode of a beggar-saint or mendicant).

3. The formative influences of the Brahmin Guru Venkusha and his *ashram* at Sailu on Babu for twelve years from his age of 4 to 16, were most significant. The Guru moulded Him into the type of unique saint that He emerged by his teachings, blessings and bestowal of special grace or power. Sri Shirdi Sai Baba acknowledged the greatness of His Guru Venkusha and the deep debt He owed to him for all the love and grace that he showered on Him. Besides Guru Venkusha, the influence of His pir group in the *ashram* also had its affect. Babu (adolescent Baba) served His teacher with total devotion and utmost love and Guru Venkusha, therefore, loved him most. This had caused jealousy in the hearts of a number of boys who were all the time trying to browbeat Him and ultimately one day overpowered and hit Him with a brick on His forehead in the forest. Baba did not harbour any ill-will whatever against his peers even in such circumstances. Baba had a close friend Sukh Ram in the Guru's *ashram* at Sailu who later became known as Sakha Ram Maharaj, the great saint of Angaon Kawas, and Baba and Sukh Ram maintaind their cordial links for several decades; even though Sakha Ram never came to Shirdi, Sri Sai Baba of Shirdi miraculously manifested Himself at Sakha Ram's place many times.

4. After leaving His Guru's *ashram* in 1854, Babu, the young boy saint, reached Shirdi, stayed there for barely two months and then wandered from place to place. During this time, for some years He stayed in a mosque at Aurangabad where He instructed a Muslim *faqir* Pir Mohammed, who later on came to Shirdi and stayed with Baba during 1909-1918 and was known as *Bade Baba* who was given a big *dakshina* everyday by Baba for many years out of the *dakshina* received from devotees. Baba lived with one *faqir* Ali (perhaps Akbar Ali) in a mosque in Ahmednagar for some time. Baba once told about an old Muslim *faqir* whom He served by begging alms and food for him daily. In all probability, he was Bade Baba as mentioned above, but it is also possible that there might have been some other saint whom Baba served. Baba must have met a number of Hindu and Muslim saints during His wanderings during 1854-58 and thus assimilated the characteristics of both Hindu and Muslim saints which formed His composite and universalistic personality.

5. Baba reached Shirdi for the second time in 1858 and stayed there permanently till His *Maha Samadhi* on 15 October, 1918, that is for sixty years. During this long span of six decades, many saints came to Shirdi to have *darshan* and blessings of Baba and among them were such great saints as Gadge Maharaj, Alindi Swami, Darvesh Shah, Madhu Shah, Bal Gangadhar Tilak, etc. Many saints, who in their hearts or through their intiution knew that Sri Shirdi Sai Baba was then the greatest spiritual power on earth, sent their devotees to seek the *darshan* and blessings of the great master. Among them were such great spiritual luminaries as Anandswami, Yogi Kulkarni, Tembe Maharaj, Narsing Maharaj, Ramanand Bidkar Maharaj, Vaman Shashi Islampurkar, etc. A number of saints never visited Shirdi and also Baba never visited them at their *ashrams, mutts* or places physically; none sent his disciple to Baba and vice versa. But, these saints were in contact with Baba internally, spiritually and constantly. Among such saints, mention may be made of Tajuddin Baba, Sakha Ram Maharaj, Dhuniwale Dada, Vishnudevanand Saraswati, Banne Mian, Shamsuddin Faqir, Bannu Mai, Baba Jan, etc. Baba Himself sent His messages, gifts and blessings to some saints like Banne Mian and Shamsuddin Faqir. Then there were a number of saints like Ramana Maharshi, Akkalkot Swami, Guru Gholap, etc., who had such invisible yet deep spiritual identification with Baba that Baba appeared in the form of these saints to their devotees when they visited Shirdi and looked at Baba or His photograph placed in *Gurusthan*. It must also be noted that another category of saints were drawn to Baba as His devotees, later to emerge great saints due to Baba's grace, guidance and divine help although they were only young or middle-aged devotees in Baba's time, they later became known as great saints.

6. Baba had made two declarations about His role as a guru:

   i) I do not instruct through the ear (I do not give *mantra*), our traditions are different; and

   ii) I have no disciples in this world, I have countless devotees. You do not recognise in the distinction between a disciple and a devotee. Anyone can be a devotee, but that is not the case with the disciple. ...a disciple is one who carries out implicitly the commands of the Guru. The mark of the *shishya* is total devotion to the preceptor (Guru). Only the man who says, 'I have none in the world other then the preceptor, is a disciple.

Even then, some of His devotees greatly benefitted from Baba by spiritual contact and became great saints in course of years — Upasani Maharaj became an eminent saint mainly due to Baba's training. Mention ought to be made of Abdul, Das Ganu, Sai Sharananand, Megha, Bhisma, Mlahaspati, Shivamma Thayee, Hemadpant, Mataji Krishnapriyaji and some others who belong to this privileged category of Sai Baba's contemporary saints — His devotee-saints.

No Nana, I do not do any miracles. You have village astrologers. They work 2 or 4 days ahead and give out their predictions. Some of them come true. I look further ahead. My art is also a sort of astrology. But you people do not understand this. To you, My words look like chamatkar, because you do not know the future. So you regard events as proofs of miracle-working power and you turn your reverence onto Me. I, in My turn, turn your reverence onto God and see that you are really benefited.

—Sri Shirdi Sai Baba

9

Thrilling Miracles

SRI Shirdi Sai Baba was an incarnation of Lord Shiva. He possessed all *siddhis* and miraculous powers, but rarely displayed them. According to Sri Sathya Sai Baba:

> He (Sri Shirdi Sai Baba) was a *Poornavatar* (full incarnation). He had all the attributes of divine *Shakti* (power) but held them in check and did not reveal these fully. He was like a learned musician who exhibited his musical skill occasionally; He was like a gifted poet who gave voice to his verse only rarely; He was like a skilled sculptor who only revealed his artistry sometime.
>
> ...*Siddhis* (miracles) and *leelas* (sport) were merely outpourings of His love for His devotees. They were not meant to attract but only to safeguard and protect. He did not use them like visiting cards. He used His *Shakti* only to save His devotees from distress and not for their own sake but as a means of protecting the devotees from harm and danger. But even so, the full potential of His divine *Shakti* was not revealed.

Countless miracles done by Shirdi Sai Baba have been reported in the Sai literature. The first miracle done by Him was as child Babu of 5 years of age at Manwat village where He lived with the widowed wife of a Muslim *faqir*. He had swallowed the *saligram* (worship stone) of a *Sahukar's* family having won it in a game of marble from the *Sahukar's* son. "When the *Sahukar's* wife compelled Babu (Baba's childhood

Thrilling Miracles

name) to open His mouth, she saw in it the *vishwaroopa,* worlds rolling on worlds." Babu laughingly said that the *saligram* was in the worship room. She ran back there and found the *saligram* in its place in her house. She had now realised that He was divine."

At the age of 16, on the last day at His Guru Venkusha's *ashram* at Sailu, on Venkusha's instructions Babu (Baba) performed a thrilling miracle of bringing back to life the dead body of His *ashram* mate who had hit Baba with a brick on the forehead in the forest near Sailu and who had then suddenly died some minutes earlier. This miracle was performed by Baba in 1854, a few days before His first move to Shirdi.

Just a few days prior to His second move to Shirdi in 1858, Baba performed three miracles before Chand Bhai Patil in the forest near the twin villages of Sindhon-Bindhon, materialising live amber and water for his *chilum* (pipe) and then showing to him his lost mare Bijli grazing grass near a stream. These miracles are very widely known to all Sai devotees. However, most people do not know two other thrilling miracles performed by Baba when He reached Chand Bhai Patil's village Dhoop Kheda after 2-3 days on Chand Bhai Patil's invitation. The village crowd, curious to see the young *faqir* (Baba) when Chand Bhai was escorting Him from the village boundary towards his house, became restive and started pushing and pinching Him. Thereupon, Baba started hurling stones at the crowd in all directions to disperse it. Two of the stones hit a lame boy and a mad girl of about 12 years who used to roam about naked. They both were immediately cured of their ailments and the villagers were later thrilled to find these miraculous cures done by Baba.

During His long stay at Shirdi for 60 years from 1858 to 1918, Shirdi Sai Baba performed countless miracles. Only some of these have been recorded in *Shri Sai Sat Charita, Devotees Experiences of Sri Sai Baba,* Khaparde's *Shirdi Diary* and Sai Sharnananda's *Sri Sai The Superman* and *Sri Sai Baba.* Thousands of miracles experienced by innumerable visitors and residents of Shirdi during Baba's lifetime have actually gone unreported. Shivamma Thayee's experiences, for example, could not thus be brought to the notice of the public as they did not find mention in the above books. It is now impossible to collect even a part of all the miracles perfomed by Baba. However, on the basis of miracles reported in these books, we find that Baba's miracles were of various kinds. They may be broadly classified as under:

1. *Baba's Miraculous Materialisations:* Baba materialised holy water streams flowing from His toes for Das Ganu. Ganu recalled the incident in these words:

Baba knew my mentality and asked me to approach His feet and hold my palm near the feet. The water began to flow from both His feet. It was not a few drops like perspiration. It was rather a slow and thin current. In short time, say few minutes, I had collected a palmful of that water. Here was Ganges and I was delighted.

Baba materialised live amber and water for his *chilum* before Chand Bhai Patil as already mentioned. He materialised water for one of his thirsty devotees walking on a hilly tract.

2. *His Miraculous Cures of Disease and Infertility:* Baba cured innumerable patients of all kinds of diseases like dysentery, fever, smallpox, cholera, leprosy, etc. He blessed many barren women and gave them his famous *udi* (holy ash) from his *dhuni* or a coconut or mango and they gave birth to children within a year. To a devotee, Damodar Rasane, Baba gave four mangoes to be given to his junior wife to be eaten. Rasane testified as under:

I had two (wives), both living when I went to Baba. I had consulted astrology. *Ketu* was in the fifth place in the horoscope and so there was the difficulty of getting issue. But Baba, a *Satpurush,* overcame all that. He anticipated and provided for the issue after so many years. He said 8 children will be born to my younger wife, to whom I was to give the four mango fruits He gave me.

3. *His Miraculous Cures of Blindness:* Baba cured some people of their blindness. In 1916. He gave eyesight to the grandfather of Vithal Rao V. Deshpande. One blind person requested Baba, "Please grant me eyesight till I satiate my eyes to behold Your human form; and You may withdraw this grant of eyesight as soon as that is done." Sai Sharanananda reports: "Baba at once granted this request; he saw Baba with his own eyes and then lost his vision and became blind." Sharananand has reported about a blind man whom he saw during Baba's time at Shirdi, but who was found reading religious books in 1942-43; evidently he had regained his eyesight by Baba's grace.

4. *His Miraculous Cure of Snake Poisoning:* In those days Shirdi was full of snakes and Baba cured a number of people including His close devotee Shama. "He stopped the spread of poison of the serpent's fang simply by His command to the serpent and keeping Madhav Rao (Shama) awake the whole night chewing *neem* leaves." When a scorpion stung Bapu Saheb Jog, Baba simply said, "Go, the pain will soon vanish."

5. *His Miraculous Grace of Showering Property on the Needy:* By His miraculous blessing, many people like Sant Ashram, Sant Gadge Maharaj, Anwar Khan Kazi of Ahmedabad and many others miraculously found fund to complete their contemplated projects of building temple, *dharamshalas* and mosque respectively. How thrilling is Imam Bhai Chote Khan's testimony in this connection:

> Anwar Khan Kazi of Ahmednagar wanted to rebuild a *masjid* at Teliakoot (Kajichi Masjid). He came to Baba for funds. Baba told him (after he waited long) that the *masjid* would not accept any money from him or others, but would herself provide the funds. "Dig 3 feets under the *nimbar* and you will find a treasure. Rebuild the *masjid* with that," said Baba. Then the Kazi went to Ahmednagar, found the treasure, rebuilt and came to Shirdi and when seated in the *takia* here told me and others of the above facts. As for Baba's telling him the above I was present then. Baba was seated on the big stone in front of the mosque.

Baba directed some others to dig the ground under some trees or where they passed stools to find treasure. He gave a packet covered in paper to someone and asked him to open it only at his house. While coming to a river on the way, he could not resist the temptation of opening the parcel to see its contents, and finding in it a piece of mutton, he at once threw it in the river but soon lamented on seeing it turning into gold in water.

Imam Bhai Chote Khan has recorded another thrilling incident:

> A Moslem from Lasoor in Nizam's state (Taluk Vyzapur) came to Baba some 27 years ago (around 1913) and cried wanting Rs. 4,000 or Rs. 5,000 to meet some urgent need. Baba told him to go and sit under the *vat* tree to ease himself, where a vessel full of coins would be found by him. Next morning, he did as directed and stumbled upon a very heavy vessel evidently full of treasure. He could not lift it and so he came to Baba at *Chavadi.* When he returned, it had disappeared, so he cried. Baba said Ganu Kadu of Ruiyad had carried it away and so nothing could be done. That Ganu Kadu is a rich man and the Lasoor man went back in grief.

6. *His Blessings to People for Jobs, Success in their Ventures:* In 1912, Baba blessed that Narke would get service in Poona several years before it materialised in 1918. Baba blessed an unemployed man and he became a teacher. Baba advised his devotees like Rasane not to sow a certain crop, not to do a certain business and thus saved them from future

losses. Those who did not follow His advice, very soon suffered great misfortunes.

7. *His Protection:* Baba seated in Dwarka Mai Masjid saved the life of a blacksmith's baby son who had accidently fallen in the burning furnace from the lap of his mother; Baba's hand got burnt in a miraculous manner while saving that child. He saved a number of His devotees from thieves, robbers, fire, floods, and other accidents.

8. *His Control on the Forces of Nature:* On many occasions of storm or heavy rain, Baba just asked the clouds to "Go away" or *"Bas kar, ab ja"* (That's all; now go) and they glided away, clearing the sky instantly. Baba saved the inhabitants of Shirdi from plague by getting flour gounded on the village boundary.

9. *Instant Knowledge of People's Thoughts, Conversation, Action, etc.:* Innumerable devotees and visitors have testified to the facts of Baba's omniscience. Baba knew everything spoken or thought of by His devotees and visitors even hundreds of miles away and He thrilled countless persons by responding in such a manner as to expose their secrets instantly.

10. *Protection to Visitors Coming to Shirdi and Returning to their Homes.*

11. *Miraculous Materializing of a Horse Carriage, Horse, Carriage driver, Servant to Carry His Messenger Ramgir Bua to Nana's House at Jamner.*

12. *Miracles Before His Visitors:* Turning seedy grapes into seedless grapes; turning sour lemon drink into a sweet drink, burning earthen lamps in the Dwarka Mai Masjid with water when local merchants refused to give oil.

13. *Knowledge of the Several Births and Future Births of His Devotees* like Shama, Nana Saheb, Upasani Maharaj, Tatya, Laxmi, Bayja Bai, Hemadpant, several animals, insects and other creatures. There are scores of such evidence in the Sai literature.

14. *Yogic Experiences In Shri Sai Sat Charita,* Baba's miraculous yogic feet of *Khand Yoga* is described as in *Shri Sai Sat Charita:*

> In this practice, Baba revealed the various limbs of His body and strew them separately at different places in the *masjid*. Once a gentleman went to the *masjid* and saw the limbs of Baba lying here and there. He was much terrified and he first thought of running to the village officers and informing them about Baba having been

hacked to pieces and murdered. He thought he would be held responsible as he was the first informant and knew something of the affair. So he kept quiet. But next day when he went to the *masjid*, he was very much surprised to see Baba, hale and hearty and sound as before.

Shivamma Thayee (then known as Rajamma Gounder) also witnessed this miracle of Baba at Shirdi in 1915. Her memoir in this connection is very thrilling:

On one of my visits to Shirdi when I was about 23-24 years old, i.e. around 1915, I witnessed a very horrible thing. I was staying in a rented room very close to Dwarka Mai. There was no latrine in that house. One night at about 1.30 a.m. I wanted to go out to urinate and for that I had to go a little far ahead in the open space crossing the Dwarka Mai where Baba slept. It was pitch dark. As I walked near Dwarka Mai in the street something like a wooden log struck my foot. I took it up. To my horror, it was a leg of the human body with blood. I put it down at once and in fear moved ahead. After only about 5-6 feet, I hit upon another mutilated part of the human body — it was a full arm cut off from the shoulder. Walking further, at a distance of 7 to 8 feet a complete leg was found by me. I was dreadfully frightened. I at once ran to my bedroom and closed the door immediately. The thought that came into my mind was that someone had murdered Sai Baba and mutilated His limbs and thrown them there in the street near the *masjid*. In the morning the police would come to investigate and there will be a lot of hue and cry in the village. Thereafter, I could not sleep at all and was silently weeping and crying in my heart. At about 5 a.m. a crow cawed. I got up from my bed and mustered some courage to peep through the window of my room. To my amazement, I saw Sai Baba sitting in the open courtyard smoking His *chilum*. Then I at once went to Baba and narrated to Him my most hair-raising experience of the night in a choked voice.

Baba then told me, "Daughter Rajamma. I had done my *Khand Yoga* last night which I sometimes do. I separate my limbs from my physical body and then my physical life is no more there. My Soul (Spirit) had seen you moving in the street and stumbling against My mutilated legs and hand but I did not speak to you because, firstly, My physical body was dead as My limbs lay scattered, and secondly, although My Spirit was mutely observing your movement in the street I could not talk to you; I chose not to give you any assurance or sign of my presence there, lest you should be frightened in that pitch dark night. I will teach you also this *Khand Yoga* shortly."

I told Baba, "I don't want to practise it." Thus I refused Shirdi Sai Baba's offer to teach me *Khand Yoga*.

Shivamma Thayee had also witnessed Baba taking out his intestines, washing them, spreading them on the forewalls of the well, and then swallowing them back. This sort of incident is also recorded in *'Shri Sai Sat Charita*.

15. *Baba's Cooking by Stirring the Boiling Contents of the Big Pot with His Right Arm.*

16. *Baba's Miracle of Assuming the Forms of Various Gods and Saints:* On various occasions, Baba miraculously appeared as Lord Dattatreya, Lord Rama, Lord Krishna, Vithal, Samartha Akkalkot, Guru Gholap, etc., before His devotees and visitors. He appeared in the form of the divine three-headed child Dattatreya in the evening of Datta Jayanti in 1911 to Balwant Kohojkar. His son has recalled that incident in these words:

During his (my father Balwant Kohojkar's) stay at Shirdi in 1911, Datta Jayanti occurred. About 5 p.m. or so, Baba was seated at the mosque with devotees around Him. At once He said, "I am having the pangs of labour. I cannot bear it. I am about to be delivered." Evidently, He was identifying Himself with Anasuya, mother of Datta, who at that time had her pains of labour and was undergoing sympathetic pain. At twilight (i.e., shortly after the above incident), He sent out all people from the mosque and again after a little while He called the people to come to Him. Then He was in glee. All the people went in and among them my father directly entered the mosque; what he saw on Baba's seat and in place of Baba's figure was a small child, a charming three-faced figure of Datta (Datta as an infant). That view he saw just for a moment. Then, instead of Datta's figure, he saw at the identical spot Baba in His usual dress and form." Sri Sathya Sai Baba has also vividly corroborated this incident of Kohojkar witnessing Sri Shirdi Baba's miracle of turning into Datta, while giving his discourse on September 27, 1992.

17. *Help to Students:* In 1917, an examinee of a medical course saw a dream. In the dream Baba told him, "I am having very serious pain in my stomach. Search out a suitable medicine and give it to Me." Next day, he found a similar question in the question paper. Similarly, Baba blessed and helped the students of Shirdi Primary School when they went to seek

Thrilling Miracles

His blessings to face the examination to be given by the visiting Inspector of schools. Baba predicted to an examinee that his roll No. 114 would certainly appear in the list of successful candidates. He prophesied to another candidate that he would not pass that year no matter how much he prepared, but next year he would pass. Many such miracles must have happened to innumerable candidates and gone unreported.

18. *Miracles of Baba's Resurrection:* In 1886, Baba left for His heavenly abode, stayed there for three days and then again became alive. After attaining *Maha Samadhi* on October 16, 1918, He resurrected at His devotee Mathaji Krishna Priya's cottage at Simla as revealed by Sri Sathya Sai Baba in His discourse on October 6, 1992:

She, Mataji Krishna Priya (Baba's devotee from Nagpur), came to know that Baba had left His mortal shell at 2.30 p.m. on *Vijaya Dashmi* day in 1918. Immediately after this *Ekadasi* followed.... Krishna Priya came to know of this and felt very sad the whole day. The next day (October 16, 1918) she closed all the doors and windows of her house because of the severe cold in Simla. While she was resting in the house, a tall and well built monk arrived at the next door and enquired about Mataji's house. He made enquiries not because he did not know where Mataji lived, but only to make others know that He was physically present in Simla. The neighbours sent a servant with an umbrella as it was snowing, to show the stranger Mataji's house. He knocked at the door. Mataji opened the door and could not believe what her eyes were seeing. She wondered how Baba, who had passed away the previous day, could come to Simla. She asked, "How did you manage to come so soon?" It takes at least three days to come from Shirdi to Simla. Baba said, *"Beti"* (daughter), I am everywhere. You have worshipped Me in the form of Krishna. Is this all that you know about Me? I am feeling the cold, first give Me hot tea." She prepared the tea and offered it to Baba. After taking the tea, Baba said that He was hungry after His long journey. Krishna Priya brought Him chapatis and brinjal curry that Baba used to like very much. After taking the food Baba washed His hands and wiped them on a towel. He then told her, "The purpose for which I came is over and I am going away." He gave her a jasmine garland. Krishna Priya watched Him as He went away walking through the bazaar. In Simla, on the roadside there are deep valleys. As Baba was walking along, some workmen were engaged in some road work. Noting that Baba had fallen down on the road, they ran to rescue Him. But they could find nobody there. Baba had just disappeared.

19. Baba's Unique Miracles of Saving a Captain of a Ship in Sea and a Girl who had Fallen in Well at Shirdi: Baba miraculously saved Jahangir Framaji Daruwala, captain of a ship, from drowning in the sea. Sai Sharanand has narrated the miracle thus:

...Baba had run to the rescue of three steamers of His devotees during the Russo-Japanese war. The devotee, Shree Jahangirji Framaji Daruwala, served as a captain. When he was told that his steamers save three were all sunk by the enemy and that the rest of the steamers including his own would soon meet the same fate, he took out Baba's photo from his pocket and with tears in his eyes prayed to Baba to save him and his three steamers. Baba at once appeared on the scene and towed all the sinking steamers to the bank. Just at the time Daruwala offered his prayers, Baba called out "Ha," and then seated as He was in His usual place in Dwarka Mai he had his *kafni* and head cloth completely drenched, dripping water for more than half an hour, with the result that the Dwarka Mai was transformed into a pool of water. The devotees could not understand what it all was: they simply removed water from Dwarka Mai and dried Baba's clothes. On the third day after this Baba received a telegram from Jehangirji narrating how Baba had saved him and offering Him a thousand thanks for His marvellous rescue of himself and his three steamers with passengers. Immediately on return to India he came and paid his respects to Baba.

Baba saved the three years old daughter of Babu Kirwandikar who had fallen into the well in Shirdi, but mysteriouly Baba held her suspended in mid-air.

Once Baba and three of His devotees were eating their lunch in the Dwarka Mai Masjid. Baba suddenly said, "Stop!" Then they continued with their lunch. Soon after they had finished and cleared out of the *masjid,* large chunks of the ceiling fell on the very spot where they had been seated only a few minutes earlier.

20. Baba's Granting Detachment or Spirituality by His Mere Touch: In the Sai literature, a few instances have been discovered by us — when Baba granted the wishes of His devotees for attaining detachment or spirituality merely by His divine penetrating looks or special touch.

In about 1915, when he (Abul Kadir) was here at the *takia,* Baba passed by that side. Kadir then begged of Baba to give him *faqiri* as he wanted to become a saint. Baba then flung His folded palm at him as though He held something in it and was flinging the same at him.

But there was nothing visibly held in Baba's hand. Thereafter Kadir's manner and talk changed. He gave moral advice and behaved like Baba...

Sant Narayan Ashram's memoirs of Baba contain this insightful observation:

Baba had a way of touching (with His palm) the head of the devotee who went to Him. There was no *adhikari* evident to anything that Baba could give and thus there was none to succeed His position. But His touch did convey certain impulses, forces, ideas, etc. Sometimes He pressed His hand heavily on His head as though He was crushing out some of the lower impulses of the devotee. Sometimes He tapped, sometimes He made a pass with the palm, etc. Each had its own effect — making remarkable difference in the sensations or feelings of the devotee. Baba's touch was one means. Apart from that, He would invisibly operate on the nature of the devotee and effect a great change.

21. *Mysterious Control on Supernatural Beings and Ghosts:* Baba's ardent devotee, Professor Narke has left behind this testimony:

To one deeply observing Him, the startling fact came out in greater and greater prominence that Baba was living and operating in other worlds also, besides this world and in an invisible body.

...Baba was frequently talking of His travels with an invisible body across great distances of space. In the morning, sitting near His *dhuni* (fire) with several devotees He would say to what distant place he went overnight and what He had done.... He had travelled to distant places in an invisible form and rendered help there. Again He would talk of *post-mortem* experiences.

A Shirdi Marwadi's boy fell ill and died. People returned from the funeral to the *masjid* with gloomy faces. Sai Baba then said of that boy, "He must be nearing the river now, just crossing it." I felt that the reference could only be to *Vaitarni* (river in heaven).

Conclusion

It may be pointed out that although Sri Shirdi Sai Baba performed so many miracles He did not perform any of these for His own use. He Himself suffered from asthma from 1885 or so, and in 1915 had an acute attack, yet He did not cure Himself by His own miraculous cures. He Himself went out for begging alms even at the old age of 80, although He could easily materialise food or anything. He performed all His miracles for the protection and welfare of His devotees and visitors.

His miracles continue to happen with countless devotees throughout the world even now. People in need earnestly remember Him at the hour of their need and He instantly provides His miraculous help to them. Sometimes He appears in His usual form or in the form of any other saint, beggar, unknown person or creature but the earnest devotee is certainly enabled to recognise Him when His grace falls on him or her. Innumerable books and journals published by Sai devotees throughout the world are overflowing with accounts of many such thrilling miracles of Baba in the post-*Samadhi* years.

> *If anyone does any evil unto you, do not retaliate. If you can do anything, do something good to others.*
> —Sri Shirdi Sai Baba

10

Unique Teachings

SRI Shirdi Sai Baba was a unique Saint in many ways. Although He did not deliver long discourses and did nothing to show Himself as a scholar or a highly learned man yet whatever little He spoke to teach, guide or spiritualise His devotees, these are indeed unique teachings of the great divine incarnation of this *Kali* age. The particular characteristic of His teachings was that He could convey the precious contents of His teachings in such forceful, direct, unambiguous few words that even an illiterate person coming from a rural background could very easily understand and assimilate.

A careful search of *Shri Sai Sat Charita* for all the words of Sai Baba's teachings has given us 54 gems.

Precious Sayings of Sri Shirdi Sai Baba

1. *Action (Karma)*
This *deha prarabdha* (present fate) is the result of the *karma* (action) done by you in the former births.

2. *Assurance*
If a man utters My name with love, I shall fulfil all his wishes and increase his devotion. If he sings earnestly My life and deeds, him I shall beset in front and back and on all sides.

3. *Beauty*
We have not to bother about beauty or ugliness of the person, but to concentrate solely on God underlying that form.

4. Charity
The donor gives, that is, sows his seeds, only to reap a rich harvest in future. Wealth should be means to work out *Dharma*. If it is not given before, you do not get it now. So, the best way to receive is to give.

5. Contentment
One must rest content with one's lot.

6. Dakshina
The giving of *dakshina* (reverential gift) advances *vairagya* (non-attachment) and thereby *bhakti* (devotion).

7. Death
None dies; see with your inner eyes. Then you will realise that you are God and not different from Him. Like wornout garments the body is cast away.

8. Disillusion
Whenever any idea of joy or sorrow arises in your mind, resist it. Do not give room to it. It is pure disillusion.

9. Destiny
Whosoever is destined to be struck will be struck. Whosoever is to die will die. Whosoever is to be caressed will be caressed.

10. Discrimination
There are two sorts of things — the good and the pleasant. Both these approach man for acceptance. He has to think and choose one of them. The wise man prefers the good to the pleasant but the unwise, through greed and attachment, chooses the pleasant and thereby cannot gain *Brahma gyana* (self-realisation).

11. Devotee
He who withdraws his heart from wife, child and parents and loves Me is My real lover or devotee and he merges in Me like a river in the sea.

12. Devotion
Knowledge of the *Vedas* or fame as a great *jnani* (learned scholar) or formal *bhajan* (worship) are of no avail unless they are accompanied by *bhakti* (devotion).

13. Differences
People differentiate between themselves and others, their properties with other's properties. This is wrong. I am in you and you are in Me. Meditate on the self with a question "Who am I?"

14. Duty
Unless a man discharges satisfactorily and disinterestedly the duties of his station in his life, his mind will not be purified.

15. Egoism
The teachings of a Guru are of no use to a man who is full of egoism and who always thinks about sense-objects.

16. Enemy
Who is whose enemy? Do not say of anyone that he is your enemy. All are one and the same.

17. Equanimity
Let the world go topsy-turvy, you remain where you are. Standing or staying at your own place, look calmly at the show of all things passing before you.

18. Exploitation
Nobody should take the labour of others *gratis*. The worker should be paid his dues promptly and liberally.

19. Feeding
Know for certain that he who feeds the hungry, really serves Me with food. Regard this as an axiomatic truth.

20. Food
Sitting in the *masjid* (mosque) I shall never, never speak untruth. Take pity on Me like this : first give bread to the hungry and eat yourself. Note this well.

21. Forbearance
Our *Karma* is the cause of happiness and sorrow. Therefore, put up with whatever comes to you.

22. God
God lives in all beings and creatures, whether they be serpents or scorpions. He is the greatest wirepuller of the world, and all beings, serpents, scorpions, etc., obey His command.

23. *God's Gifts*
What a man gives does not last long and it is always imperfect. But what my *sircar* (God) gives, lasts to the end of life. No other gift from any man can be compared to His.

24. *God's Grace*
You must always adhere to truth and fulfil all the promises you make. Have *shraddha* (faith) and *saburi* (patience). Then I will always be with you wherever you are.

25. *God's Will*
Unless God wills it, nobody meets us on the way; unless God wills, nobody can do any harm to others.

26. *Goodness*
If you act in a good way, good will really follow.

27. *Greed*
Greed and Brahma are poles asunder; they are eternally opposed to each other. Where there is greed, there is no room for thought or meditation of the Brahma. Then how can a greedy man get dispassion and salvation?

28. *Guru*
Stick to your own Guru with unabated faith, whatever the merits of other gurus and however little the merits of your own.

29. *Guru's Grace*
The mother tortoise is on one bank of the river and her younger ones are on the other. She gives neither milk nor warmth to them. Her mere glance gives them warmth. The young ones do nothing but remember (meditate upon) their mother. The tortoises glance is, to the young ones, a downpour of nectar, the only source of sustenance and happiness. Similar is the relationship between the Guru and his disciples.

30. *Humility*
Humility is not towards all. Severity is necessary in dealing with the wicked.

31. *Happiness*
If others hate us, let us take to *Nama Japa* (chanting of God's name) and avoid them. Do not bark at people; do not be pugnacious. Bear with others' reproach. This is the way to happiness.

Unique Teachings

32. Help
If someone begs of anything and if that be in your hand or power and if you can grant the request, give it. Do not say, 'no'. If you have nothing to give them, give a polite negative reply but do not mock or ridicule the applicant nor get angry with him.

33. Hospitality
No one comes to us without *rinanubandha* (some previous bond of give and take). So when any dog, cat, pig, fly or person approaches you, do not drive it or him away with the words 'Hat - Hat', 'Jit - Jit'

34. Inquiry
Inquire always : Who am I?

35. Introspection
We must see things for ourselves. What good is there in going about asking for this man or that for his views and experiences?

36. Liberation
Service at the feet of Guru is essential to attain *moksha* (liberation).

37. Lust
A person who has not overcome lust cannot see (realise) God.

38. Name Chanting
If you do this - chanting 'Raja Ram', your mind will attain peace and you will be immensely benefited.

39. Non-possession
Everything belongs to us for use. Nothing is for us to possess.

40. Omnipresence
I am not confined within this body of three and a half cubic height; I am everywhere. See Me in every place.

41. Oneness
The dog which you saw before meals and to which you gave the piece of bread is one with Me, so also other creatures (cats, pigs, flies, cows, etc.) are one with Me. I am roaming in their forms. So abandon the sense of duality and serve Me as you did today (by feeding that dog).

42. Poverty
Poverty is the highest of riches and superior to Lord's position. God is brother of the poor. *Faqir* is the real Emperor. *Faqir* does not perish, but empire is soon lost.

43. Quarrel
If anybody comes and abuses you or punishes you, do not quarrel with him. If you cannot endure it, speak a simple word or two, or else go away from that place. But do not battle with him and behave like this.

44. Questioning
Mere questioning is not enough. The question must not be made with any improper motive or attitude or to trap the Guru and catch him at mistakes in the answer, or out of idle curiosity. It must be with a view to achieving *moksha* or spiritual progress.

45. Reality
Brahma is the only 'Reality' and the Universe is ephimeral and no one in this world, be he son, father or wife, is really ours.

46. Saints
Daily take *darshan* of *Siddhas*, i.e., perfect saints. Live a moral life. Then you will be pure even in death.

47. Self-realisation
The idea that "I am the body" is a great disillusion, and attachment to this idea is the cause of bondage. Leave this idea and therefore the attachment, if you want to reach the goal of self-realisation.

48. Service
Seva is not rendering service while still retaining the feeling that one is free to offer or refuse service. One must feel that he is not the master of the body, that the body is Guru's and exists merely to render service to Him.

49. Sin
Inflicting pain on others by body, mind and speech is sin, the reverse is merit, good.

50. Support
Come what may, stick to your Support, i.e., Guru, and ever remain steady, always in union with Him.

51. Surrender
It is My special characteristic to free any person who surrenders completely to Me and who does worship Me faithfully and who remembers Me and meditates on Me constantly.

52. Truth
You should have truth always with you. Then I will be always with you, wheresoever you are and at all times.

53. Unity
Rama and Rahim were one and the same; there was not the least difference between them; then why should their devotees fall out and quarrel among themselves? You ignorant folk, children, join hands and bring both communities together, act sanely and thus you will gain your object of national unity.

54. Vicissitudes of Life
Gain and loss, birth and death, are in the hands of God. But how blindly people forget that God looks after life as long as it lasts!

55. Wordly Honour
Do not be deluded by worldly honour. The form of the deity should be firmly fixed in the mind. Let all the senses and mind be ever devoted to the worship of the Lord.

Another mine of Sri Shirdi Sai Baba's teachings was discovered in the form of Sai Sharananand's Marathi book *Sri Sai Baba* (1982). In its chapter 17, entitled *Sai Vani,* Swami Sharananand has presented Sai Baba's original words of teaching. Baba used to speak in Marathi language and Sai Sharananand had actually lived with Him for some months, heard Him talking to devotees and giving them His words of advice. Therefore, Baba's words of advice or teachings in their rustic flavour of Marathi of the masses and Hindustani language (mixture of Hindi, Urdu, Marathi, etc.) are not only very attractive but they penetrate our minds, hearts and souls instantly like arrows.

Some of the words of advice of Baba in their original Marathi and Hindustani words — the actual words which Baba uttered to communicate in his heart-to-heart advice to His devotees for the sake of their welfare — are reproduced below:

God
1. *Allah malik hai, Dusra koi nahin. Tyachi karni alaukik, amaulik, akal a' he.*

"God is the master, None else is the master. His actions are supernatural, invaluable and full of wisdom."

    2.   *Gharibon ka Allah wali hai. Allah se bada koi nahin.*

"God is the friend of the poor. There is none greater than *Allah* (God)."

    3.   *Ishwar aahe hai, satya maan*
         Ishwar nahin hai, khote samajh,
         Sab Allah hi Allah hai,
         Ha Sarva Allah Mian cha aahe.

" 'God does exist' - consider it as truth,
'There is no God' - consider it as false;
Everything is God,
Everything belongs to God."

God's-realization
    4.   *Dev kinnai lai kanvalu aahe, aapnach tyachyawar bharosa thewit nahin aani saburi pakrit nahin.*

"It is not easy to realise God. Patience and strong determination are necessary to have the *darshan* of God."

Brevity in Speech
    5.   *Jyachyawar eshwari kripa hote to bolte nahin;*
         Pan jyachyawar eishwari avkripa hote to phaar bolte.

"Whoever is bestowed with the kindness of God does not speak; but absence of God's kindness makes a person speak unnecessarily."

On Himself
    6.   *Ham kisike bande nahin hain. Allah ke banda hain.*

"We are (I am) not servant of anyone; we are the servant of God."

    7.   *Ham Gangapur mein bhi hain, Pandarpur mein bhi hain, sab thikana mein hain, sab jagah pe Ham hain aur Hamare paas sab jag hai.*

"We are (I am) at Gangapur, We are at Pandarpur, We are at all places, and all places are with Us."

Detachment
    8.   *Dunya ikadchi tikre jhali tari apan maage pude hou nahin. Nishchal rahun kautuk teware pahawe. (Sakshiwat raha).*

Unique Teachings

"All the world is full of pulls or problems, you keep on your path, remain unmoved by the curiosity; remain detached."

Poverty

9. *Gharibi awal baadshahi, amiri se lakh sawai,*
   Gharibon ke Allah bhai.

"Poverty is first class kingship, it is better than richness, Allah is the brother of the poor."

Proper Conduct

10. *Aakalaya gelebyacha aadar kar, trishitaala paani de, bhukelyas bhakr, udharvyas wastar, wa ghar naslelyas basawyas ausri dyavi mahanje shribari tusht hoil.*

"Welcome whosoever comes to your house, give water the thirsty, cloth to the naked, keep in your house the helpless; this will satisfy Sri Hari (God)."

How to Recognise God

11. *Akkal se khuda pahchanna.*

"Recognise God with intelligence."

Actions/Karmas

12. *Achchi tarah se chalo, Allah achcha karta hai.*
    Buri tarah se chalenge to bura hota hai.

"Behave properly, Allah does good (to you). Behave improperly, then only bad will happen (to you)."

13. *Jaise jo karil, taise to bharil.*

"As you sow, so shall you reap."

14. *Neki ka phal bhari hai.*
    Badi ka phal kam hai.

"The fruit of *neki* (good actions) is heavy,
The fruit of *badi* (bad actions) is light."

15. *Jashi jyachi neeyat tashi tyachi barkat.*

"As are one's motives, so are the results of his actions."

16. *Jyacha irada changla tyache sagle chagle.*
    Aapule karam apulyasange, dujiyache to dujiya sange.

"Your actions go with you,
Others' actions go with them."

Good Conduct
17. *Konchi barobari karu nahin; Konachi ninda, konchiya bolnyane apalya karu nahin.*

"Do not compete with anyone else;
Do not speak ill of anyone else."

Contentment
18. *Woh jaisa rakhega waise rehna.*

"Live as He keeps you."

Gratitude to God
19. *Allah peksha kauni meetha nahin. To kaunya tene jeevdaan deyil? Kaunya tene sambhalil, he tyache tayalach thauk?*

"None is greater than God. Who gave you this life,
Who looked after you, Who keeps you well?"

20. *Tyachya Marjeet apan raji rahwe; talmal karu nahin. Tyachyashiwae jharache paan halat nahin.*

"We should be contented with whatever He wishes for us, we should not grudge; without God's wish not even a leaf of tree can flutter."

Duty
21. *Aaple kartwya apan karawe, pan kartepanacha aabhmaan aaplykare na gheta kartatwa parmeshwarale dhyawe, aani phal hi tyasach arpan karawe, mahanje aapn alpit rahun karam aapleyala baadhak honar nahin.*

"Everyone should do his duty without any ego, surrendering the fruit to God; thus it results in his detachment from the fruit."

Tolerance
22. *Angala bhoke parat nahit.*

"Bear whatever anybody says, for it doesn't hurt the body."

Prayer
23. *Kasht karin aasawe, tikene rahu nahin, Devache nauw dhyane, pothi puran vachawe, aahar vihar tyage nahit, pan niyamit aasawe.*

"If you are in a problem, do not sit idle lost in it; pray to God, read old scriptures, do not fast but regulate your food habits."

Unique Teachings

God's Wish
24. *Eshwar karel tech hoil, tyacha raasta toch dakhwil aani vina vilambh manachi muraad puri hoil.*

"Whatever God wishes, that will happen. He will open the door and let you enter it; He will fulfil your wishes without any delay."

Evil
25. *Bure se Khudaa dare aur Khudaa se bura dare.*

"God is afraid of evil doer, and evil doer is afraid of God."

God's Omnipotence
26. *Parameshwar aahe wa tyachya peksha kauni motha nahin.
To sarv chara-chara madhye bharun urla aahe.
Utpan nahin toch karito, rakhi tohi toch,
barhwit tohi toch, aani mari tohi toch.
To thewil tase rahawe.*

"None is greater than God who is omnipresent and omnipotent, Who has given you birth, Who has nurtured you, Who alone kills you; as He keeps you, you remain."

Love
27. *Sarv bhut matranshi premaane wagawe.
Waadawaadi karu nahin, koni kahi bolle tari ekun dhyawe.*

"Treat all with love; do not argue, do not unnecessarily talk with others, concentrate on Him."

Right thinking
28. *Pratyekane nekane waagaawe,
sadsadhichar shakti jagrit thewavi.*

"Guide everyone on the right path; develop right thinking."

Sai Messages
Although Shirdi Sai Baba achieved *Maha Nirvana* in 1918, His valuable messages are still received while in a state of meditation by a number of His real devotees. One such blessed devotee is Sri K. V. Raghavana, whose compilation of the messages received by him in dreams have been published by All India Sai Samaj (1984), Madras. Some of these thrilling messages are in continuation of the Baba's teachings in His lifetime:

1. For whom are you craving:
   You should crave for Me
   For the merger of your soul with Me;
   That is the perfect bliss
   Without sorrow. (August 1982)

2. Butterfly is delicate and short-lived;
   It sucks honey and does no harm to others.
   Man should emulate the same,
   He should suck divine honey,,
   Be harmless to others
   And make his life sweet and short-lived.
   (August 1981; Baba appeared as a butterfly to K.V.R. Rao)

3. Each life is like a rose,
   Man should emulate the rose
   The fragrance of the rose
   To be thrown open
   and not the thorn.
   God within self is the fragrance
   To be thrown open
   Through prayer. (May 1982)

4. Pain is for the body and mind
   And not for the soul;
   Try to live with the soul
   And you will be liberated. (July 1982)

5. It is difficult to please
   Everybody in all matters,
   For this only, we have to look
   For the Lord to please everybody. (November 1982)

6. Body seeks pleasure
   Soul seeks salvation
   Live with the soul
   To achieve liberation
   Liberation from the mind
   and liberation from pleasure. (December 1982)

7. *Purpose of Life*
   Human life is provided with an opportunity for rational thinking; the individual should develop the same through prayer; prayer provides the upliftment of the soul.
   (June 1983)

Unique Teachings

8. *Faith*
   Faith in God is the only anchor for the ship of *Samsar*, whether smooth or troubled waters. (August 1983)

9. *Inevitable Destiny*
   The inevitable is to be accepted by everyone specially when it is blessed by the Lord for reasons unknown to us.
   (June 1983)

10. *Rinanubandha*
    Man knows his relations in the present life and is attached to them dearly; he knows not the relationship in previous life *Rinanubandha* unless he looks to Me. (August 1983)

11. *Realisation*
    If you realise that you are not the body,
    Half the problems are solved;
    If you experience you are the soul,
    The distance to God-realisation is crossed;
    If you feel the presence of Lord,
    Your mission is fulfilled. (August 1983)

12. *Present Life*
    Whom are you blaming?
    I have created this body for you,
    To be with Me all the time
    To think of Me, pray for Me
    And, ask for Me
    Don't blame the family nor the society. (September 1983)

The teachings and messages of Sri Sai Baba are so direct, transparent and lucid that they are immediately assimilated by every person irrespective of his religion, caste, class, sex, nationality and the like. None of these teachings and messages smacks of fundamentalism or parochialism; none of them portrays the zeal of a religious propagandist and his intense wish to proselytise or convert people by terrorising them with the fear of hell or nemesis. All these teachings are essentially the finest and uniquely distilled rich contents of the spirituality and morality which all the religions, codes of good conduct and all the finest examples of culture have developed so far. These teachings give the essential quality of soothing or calming the agonies of the human heart and cementing all differences. They are truly conjunctive integrating and noble.

At the time of descent of Sri Shirdi Sai Baba on the world scene, India was groaning under the atrocities and exploitation of the British; it was seething with discontent and remorse as a result of the failure of the First Battle of India's Independence led by such great patriots as Rani Laxmi Bai of Jhansi (in whose army Sri Shirdi Sai Baba also served for a few months in 1857), Nana Phadnavees, Bahadur Shah Zafar, etc. On top of it, the mutual jealousies and disunity were eating up the very vitals of Indian society due to the poisonous cankers of casteism, Hindu-Muslim hatred, diehard ritualism and exploitation by the Brahmins. There was a serious crisis which could not be averted by either the propagation of a new religion or any movement for the mass conversion of the Hindus as the Muslim fanatics were trying or that of the Muslims to Hinduism as Swami Dayanand, a contemporary of Sri Shirdi Sai Baba, was advocating enthusiastically. These teachings of Sri Shirdi Sai Baba served as a natural, simple, rustic and magical panacea to all the moral and cultural maladies of the ailing, decaying and tormented Indian society as were His simple, rustic, unconventional, miraculous medicines and prescriptions for His devotees' physical ailments, like His famous *udi* (holy ash), *mungfali* (peanuts), crushed leaves of wild plants and the like.

The fact that all these teachings have won the appreciation of mankind from all sections of people all over the world — from simple illiterate villagers and nomads of Shirdi to the most sophisticated professors and writers and followers of philosophy, religion, spirituality and culture — bears testimony to the unique potency of these teachings which will continue to guide mankind so long as it exists on the planet earth.

> *Do not say of anyone that he is inimical. Who is whose enemy? Do not entertain ill-feeling towards anyone. All are one and the same.*
> —Sri Shirdi Sai Baba

11

The Universal Master

SAI Baba lived for 60 years at Shirdi during which period He did not move out physically to any other town or city. He never saw a railway train. He was never seen by anyone reading a book or writing anything; He never signed; He did not give long scholarly discourses on philosophy or spirituality. He did not start any new religious school of philosophy or sect. He did not make anyone His disciple or spiritual heir. Although thousands of people rushed towards Him to seek His divine grace and protection, only a few names of His close devotees, most of whom belonged to Shirdi village, are heard.

How can such a simple and humble *faqir* living in a small mosque be called a 'Universal Master'? In His own days, the villagers of Shirdi and the visitors thereto thought of Him as their local *chamatkari* (miracle maker) *faqir* having extraordinary divine powers. How more and more people in the world during the last eight decades have come to recognise His stature as a great Universal Master is indeed a topic of great importance.

Although He was born a Brahmin, yet He did not consider it worthwhile to emphasize this fact all His life. He kept people ignorant about His caste, community, and parental family. He did not choose to take up the propagation of Hindu religion as His life mission. He was an ideal secularist in the best traditions of religious harmony and unity. He treated all religions with equal respect and strove to bring about communal harmony and emotional and cultural integration among the followers of different religions. Only a genuine Universal Master such as Sri Sai Baba of Shirdi could bring Hindus, Muslims, Parsees, Christians and followers of other religions to such an ultimate and supreme realisation that all are essentially one and that is the very basis of intrinsic unity and integration among all people.

Instead of merely teaching, preaching or forcing the ideals of secularism, communal harmony and integration, He actually lived these ideals and His unique living example as such is the first testimony of His being considered as the 'Universal Master'.

These days, all kinds of religious, political and social leaders profess grand ideals of secularism, communal harmony and national integration, yet everyone knows how weak is the commitment of most of them to these ideals and what a fragile and pseudo kind of secularism, unity and integration they have been promoting in society. Even the best known among them are, at critical times, found to be exposed as the prisoners of their own parochial religious or sectarian beliefs, merely paying lip-service to these ideals. They remain Hindu, Muslim, Sikh, Jain, Christian, etc., refusing to come out of the shells of their own religious beliefs or to treat other religions on equal footing. Their tolerance is superficial, not genuine. Which Hindu religious saint or temple would allow Muslims to read the *Quran* in their temple or *ashram,* and which Muslim saint or mosque would allow the Hindus, Christians and others to read their scriptures in their mosque? Only a *Maha Purush,* the Universal Master, of the stature of Sri Shirdi Sai Baba could do so, as He did at His Dwarka Mai Masjid at Shirdi with such perfect neutrality, poise and ease that has virtually no parallel in the recorded history of human civilisation.

Anyone can read *Shri Sai Sat Charita, Devotees, Experiences of Sri Sai Baba* and Sai Sharananand's *Sri Sai Baba* (original Marathi edition) — the three most authentic original sources of information about Sri Shirdi Sai Baba. Therein the avid reader will find that Sri Sai Baba never spoke in favour of or against any religion. He was against religious consideration as such, His basic concern was ethics and good conduct as a human being.

The Universal Master Shirdi Sai Baba's overall effort was directed towards developing in His devotees moral control over their dispositions. All His informal advice and teachings to His devotees and all His thrilling parables, stories, disclosure of people's past lives and all His own life examples were aimed at one supreme goal : that of making men morally clean, inwardly strong and ever ready to face the ups and down of life, the turmoils of *sansara* or *bhavsagar* with a high sense of values and belief in the magnanimity of God who is omnipresent, omnipotent and omniscient.

Despite the fact that Shirdi Sai Baba was a divine personality possessing all supernatural powers and *siddhis* and the fact that if He wished He could certainly live, dress, eat and enjoy in a luxurious manner as many of the present-day Swamis, Acharyas and *Mathadeeshes,* etc., are doing, he preferred 'affective neutrality' — an utter disregard to the worldly possessions and facilities, showing no interest in the quality of habitation, food, dress, and no yearning to amass wealth for His *ashram* nor any desire to establish institutions or hereditary *gaddi* (seat) and things like these, which have been so current in the religious circles throughout the world.

A close perusal of Sai Baba's teachings and messages clearly reveal that instead of trying to promote the interests of any particular religion or cult or trying to introduce a new school of spirituality or religious philosophy, Shirdi Sai Baba always clearly and purely emphasised universal values like love, truth, unity, egolessness, detachment, commitment, forbearance, humility, help, hospitality, non-possession, service, surrender, etc. All the major religions and moral codes of human societies in the world have always been emphasizing these very values and they are, therefore, treated as universal values.

Shirdi Sai Baba's teachings represent a garland of carefully chosen sweetest flowers of morality and spirituality grown in the flowerbeds of different religions. He Himself advised many of His devotees to study religious scriptures like the *Yoga Vashistha,* the *Ramayana,* the *Gita,* the *Bhagavatha, Vishnu Sahsranama, Vithal Pothi, Holy Quran,* etc; references to them are there in *Shri Sai Sat Charita* and *Devotees Experiences of Sri Sai Baba.* It is also on record that when Bal Gangadhar Tilak's commentary on the *Gita* was presented to Him, instead of letting it be placed at His holy feet He lifted it up and touched His head with it saying "Such holy books have their rightful place on Our forehead, not at Our feet."

As one reads *Shri Sai Sat Charita* and *Devotees Experiences of Sri Sai Baba* page after page, one discovers Shirdi Sai Baba revealing these very spiritual truths of *Yoga Vashistha* to His devotees and visitors in very simple, rural, rustic words of Marathi and Hindustani. Rama was the paragon of virtues, the establisher of proprieties — *Maryada Purushottam.* Shirdi Sai Baba lived those values and extolled them by His living example as also through His direct, short and penetrating words of unornamented and unembellished speech. He advised His devotees to emulate the virtues of Rama and regularly sing *"Raja Ram, Raja Ram."*

He often referred to the *Gita* while advising His devotees. He emphasised *sharanagati* (total surrender) before one's Guru, which is the most important teaching of the *Gita*. In *Shri Sai Sat Charita* there is a very direct and concrete reference to it:

Nana Saheb Chandorkar was a good student of *Vedantha*. He had read the *Gita* with commentaries and was proud of his knowledge. He fancied that Baba knew nothing of all that or of Sanskrit till Baba one day pricked the bubble. These were the days before crowds flocked to Baba, when Baba had solitary talks at the mosque with the devotees. Nana was always sitting near Baba and massaging His legs and muttering something.

Baba - Nana, what are you mumbling to yourself?
Nana - I am reciting a *shloka* from Sanskrit.
Baba - What *sloka?*
Nana - From the *Bhagavatha Gita*.
Baba - Utter it loudly.

Nana then recited the *Bhagavatha Gita* (IC - 34) which is as follows:
"*Tadviddhi Pranipatena Pariprashnena Sevyaya.*
Upadeshyanto Te Jnanam Hnaniastattwaderashinah".

Baba - Nana, do you understand it?
Nana - Yes.
Baba - If you do, tell Me.
Nana - It means this -

'Making *sashtanga namaskar,* i.e., prostration, questioning the guru, serving Him, learn what this *gyana* is. Then, those *jnanis* who have attained real knowledge of the *Sad-Vastu* (Brahma) will give you *upadesha* (instruction) of *jnana*.'

Baba - Nana, I do not want this sort of collected purport of the whole stanza. Give Me each word, its grammatical force and meaning.

Then Nana explained it word by word.

Baba - Nana, is it enough to merely make prostration?
Nana - I do not know any other meaning for the world *pranipata* than making prostration.
Baba - What is *Pariprashnena?*
Nana - Asking questions.
Baba - What does *prashna* mean?
Nana - The same (questioning).
Baba - If *pariprashnena* means the same as *prashna* (questioning) why did Vyasa add the prefix *pari*. Was Vyasa off his head?

The Universal Master

Nana   - I do not know of any other meaning for the word *pariprashnena*.
Baba   - *Seva*, what sort of *seva* is meant?
Nana   - Just what we are always doing.
Baba   - Is it enough to render such service?
Nana   - I do not know what more is signified by that word *seva*.
Baba   - In the next line *upadeshyanto te jnanam*, can you so read it as to read any other word in lieu of *jnanam*?
Nana   - Yes.
Baba   - What word?
Nana   - *Ajnanam*.
Baba   - Taking that word (instead) of *jnana*, is any meaning made out of the verse?
Nana   - No, Shankara Bhashya gives no such construction.
Baba   - Never mind if he does not. Is there any objection to using the word *ajnana* if it gives a better sense?
Nana   - I do not understand how to construe by placing *Ajnana* in it.
Baba   - Why does Krishna refer Arjuna to *jnanis* or *tattwadarshi* to do his prostration, interrogation and service? Was not Krishna a *tattwadarshi*, in fact *jnana* itself?
Nana   - Yes. He was. But I do not make out why he referred Arjuna to *jnanis*.
Baba   - Have you not understood this?

Nana was humiliated. His pride was knocked on the head.

Then Baba began to explain:

i) It is not enough merely to prostrate before the *jnanis*. We must make *sarvaswa sharanagat* (complete surrender) to the Guru.

ii) Mere questioning is not enough. The question must not be asked with any improper motive to trap the Guru and catch him at mistakes in answer or out of idle curiosity. It must be serious and with a view to achieving *moksha* or spiritual progress.

iii) *Seva* is not rendering service, retaining still the feeling that one is free to offer or refuse service. One must feel that he is not the master of the body, that the body is guru's and exists merely to render service to Him. If this is done, the *Sad-guru* will show you what the *jnana* referred to in the previous stanza is.

...Baba added:

1) *Pranipata* implies surrender.
2) Surrender must be of body, mind and wealth.
3) Why should Krishna refer Arjuna to other *jnanis*? "*Sadhakas* take everything to be Vasudev (B.G. VII-19), i.e., any Guru takes a disciple to Vasudev and Krishna treats both as his *prana* and *atma*. As Sri Krishna knows that there are such *Bhaktas* and Gurus, he refers Arjuna to them so that their greatness may increase and be known.

A perusal of *Shri Sai Sat Charita* clearly bears out that Shirdi Sai Baba laid greatest emphasis on the universally acclaimed spiritual discipline of egolessness, detachment and surrender which Lord Krishna taught in the *Gita*.

Bhishma in 'Shanti Parva' of the *Mahabharata* advised the Pandavas as follows:

Truthful speech is commendable; more commendable is speech directed to do good; in my opinion that is truth which is the greatest benefit to living beings.

In Sri Shirdi Sai Baba's teachings this very concept of truthful conduct directed towards the good of others finds a place of pride. How poignant and forcefully penetrating are His following words:

You must always adhere to truth and fulfil all the promises you make. Have *shraddha* (faith) and *saburi* (patience), then I will always be with you wherever you are.

"...Restrain yourself from forbidden food and drinks. Avoid needless disputation. Avoid falsehood. Have restraint of speech."

"...You have got to make *vichar* or make enquiry about your true nature."

Universality, humanism and tolerance have been the most essential traits of *Santana Dharma*. '*Sathyam, Shivam, Sundram*' are the three highest universal values of Hinduism. The eternal question "*Who am I?*", which engaged the attention of almost all the Vedic sages and that of Ramana Maharshi, a contemporary of Shirdi Sai Baba, was also often posed by Baba to His devotees. He advised them to ponder over "Who am I?"

Ramana advised:

When other thoughts arise, one should not pursue them, but should

The Universal Master

inquire: 'To whom did they arise?' It does not matter how many thoughts arise. As each thought arises, one should inquire with diligence, "To whom has this thought arisen?" The answer that would emerge be, "To me." Thereupon if one inquires, "Who am I?", the mind will go back to its source; and the thought that arose will become quiescent. With repeated practice in this manner, the mind will develop the skill to stay in its source.... Whatever one does, one should not do with the egoity "I". If one acts in that way, all will appear as of the nature of Shiva (God)."

Shri Sai Sat Charita records an incident of a Marwadi (businessman) who had come to Shirdi Sai Baba with prayer to show him *Brahma gyan* or self-realisation. Baba's instructions to him were:

> "For seeing *Brahma gyan* one has to give five things, i.e., surrender five things: (1) Five *pranas* (vital forces); (2) Five *indriyas* (senses); (3) *mana* (mind); (4) *buddhi* (intellect); and *aham* (ego).
>
> "...How can he whose mind is engrossed in wealth, progeny and prosperity, expect to know the Brahma without removing his attachment for the same?"

Shirdi Sai Baba did not extol the virtue of one's taking *sanyas*. He advised His devotees to lead normal family lives, to live in society and yet remain detached, pure and elevated. The concept of *moksha* (liberation) is one of the most important concepts of Hinduism. For that end, several modes of worship, penance, fasts, rituals and other prescriptions like *japa, tapa* and the like have been prescribed. Shirdi Sai Baba did not want His devotees to be confused and get lost in the rigmarole of liberation but just to do these four things — to have *shraddha* (faith) and *saburi* (patience); to do *namasmaran* (name chanting), to surrender to Guru, and to do duties of one's station in life honestly and properly in a detached manner.

In Islam, the values of respect for the rights of fellow beings, equality, mercy, justice, characterfulness, piety, tolerance, peace, forgiveness, hospitality, perseverance, courage, etc., have been emphasised.

> Islam presents a very clear concept of God: "There is no God save Him, the living, the eternal. Neither slumber nor sleep overtake Him. Unto Him belongeth whatever is in the Heavens and whatever is in the earth. Who can intercede with Him save by His own leave? He knoweth that which is in front of them and that which is behind them... He is the Sublime, the Magnificent."

Let us see these teachings of Shirdi Sai Baba and we shall immediately know that they are quite identical with the Islamic values and the Islamic conception of God mentioned above:

Sitting in this *masjid* I shall never, never speak untruth. Take pity on Me like this. First give bread to the hungry, then eat yourself. Note this well. Sri Hari (God) will certainly be pleased if you give water to the thirsty, bread to the hungry, clothes to the naked and your verandah to strangers for sitting and resting.... Let anybody speak hundreds of things against you, do not resent by giving any bitter reply. If you always tolerate such things, you will certainly be happy. Let the world go topsy-turvy, you remain where you are. Standing or staying in your own place, look on calmly at the show of all things passing before you. Demolish wall of difference that separates you and Me.

..."*Allah Malik*", i.e., "Allah is the Sole Proprietor, nobody else is our Protector. His method of work is extraordinary, invaluable, and inscrutable. His will be done and He will show us the way and satisfy our heart's desires.

God is, consider it as truth,
God is not, consider this as untruth,
Everything is Allah, only Allah,
All this is Allah Mian's.

God is the Master, none else is. His actions are extraordinary and inscrutable. None is greater than Allah who gave you birth, who looked after you.

Reading these words of Baba, one feels as if Prophet Mohammed Himself was speaking through the mouth of Shirdi Sai Baba. He believed in one God and "*Allah Malik*" was His constant refrain.

Jesus Christ's two commandments 'Love of God' and 'Love of Neighbours'; and the universally acclaimed emphasis on prayer, worship and service are the greatest contributions of Christianity to humanity. This very universal value of Love found its highest culmination in the life and teachings of Shirdi Sai Baba as the Universal Master, the kind of which the world had not yet known. He not only preached but by His daily behaviour and life activities exemplified the genuine love and concern He had not only for men, women and children, but even for animals, birds and insects. Countless religious and spiritual personalities and scriptures throughout the 8,000 years old cultural history of mankind have been repeating the importance of love as a supreme human value which cements human hearts and elevates man to divinity, but none had ever given such a direct, empirical and thrilling demonstration of love in action as was done by Shirdi Sai Baba who in numerous incidents of His stunning miracles like appearing in the forms of a hungry dog, a pig, a buffalo, a beggar, a *sadhu,* an ant, insects or the like, accepted food offered by His devotees, or took over the illness, grievous wounds and scorching heat of the blacksmith's fireplace inflicted on innocent human beings and animals.

In a simple yet grand and thrilling manner, He demonstrated each time that all creatures have the same *atma* and therefore all must be loved by us as we love ourselves. As Christ used to say, "All are one, be like everyone." Shirdi Sai Baba shared His food with His devotees, dogs, cats, birds, insects freely, and loved them all equally without the least trace of differentiation. Nowhere, not even in the stories of *Puranas* which are full of all sorts of thrilling and unimaginable stories of miracles, do we come across such thrilling demonstrations of genuine love which Shirdi Sai Baba showed for the world. Indeed, there have been innumerable miracle men in the long history of mankind but Shirdi Sai Baba was the first one in the world to use His miracle-making powers to teaching illiterate and semi-literate people who could not understand the intricate scriptures, the basic principles of spirituality — the principle of *atma* common to all creatures and the principle of love. Thus Sri Shirdi Sai Baba's stature as the Universal Master legitimately and mainly rests on this sort of unprecedented exemplification or empirical evidence of the universal element or power of love on which the whole cosmos is held together and functions.

Sikhism like Islam, upholds the concept of One God, and this was also preached by Shirdi Sai Baba all His life through word and deed. Also Guru Nanak's most remarkable elucidation of Guru's importance in the life of a disciple finds its total replication in the memoirs and the teachings of Shirdi Sai Baba. The common refrain of both was that one cannot gain anything without achieving Guru's grace. Guru Nanak sang:

Without the Guru, one goes astray and transmigrates,
Without the Guru, the efforts become useless,
Without the Guru, the man serves furiously,
Without the Guru, one is not satisfied in Maya,
Without the Guru, one loses at every step, says Nanak.

Comparing this with what Shirdi Sai Baba said about Guru to His devotee Mrs Radhabai Deshmukh said:

Oh mother, my Guru never taught Me any *mantra;* then how shall I blow any *mantra* in your ears? Just remember that Guru's tortoise-like loving glance gives us happiness. Do not try to get *mantra* or *updesh* from anybody. Make Me the sole object of your thoughts and you will, no doubt, attain *paramartha* (the spiritual goal of life).... No *sadhna*, nor proficiency in the six *shastras*, are necessary. Have faith and confidence in your Guru. Believe fully that Guru is the sole *actor* or *doer*. Blessed is he who knows the greatness of his Guru and thinks him to be Hari, Hara and Brahma *(Trimurti* incarnate).

To his another devotee Pant, Baba instructed thus:

Come what may, leave not but stick to your bolster (support, i.e., Guru) and ever remain steady, always atoneness (in union) with him.

In his memoirs of Sai Baba, Professor G.G. Narke confessed as under:

According to Sai Baba traditions, the disciple or devotee that comes to the feet of the Guru in complete surrender has to be no doubt pure, chaste and virtuous.... The Guru does not teach. He radiates influence. That influence is poured in and absorbed with full benefit by the soul which has completely surrendered itself, blotting out the self.

...The Guru will lift him, endow him with higher powers, vaster knowledge and increasing realisation of truth. And the end is safe in the Guru's hands. All this was not uttered by Sai Baba at one breath to me or within my hearing, but the various hints I got from His example and dealings with many and His occasional words — when put together, amount to this.

Ram Chandra Sita Ram Dev *alias* Balabhau or Balbhat of Andheri, who had first seen Shirdi Sai Baba in 1908, asked Baba to give him *updesh* and be his *Guru.*

To him Baba said:

It is not essential that one should have a Guru. Everything is within us. What you sow, so you reap. What you give, you get. There is no need for a Guru. It is all within you. Try to listen within and follow the direction you get. We must look at ourself. That is the monitor, the Guru.

Although during the last decade of His life (1908-18), He was literally rolling in wealth as He was getting *dakshina* of about 500 to 1,000 rupees per day, yet He invariably distributed the whole of it among His devotees and beggars and poor people retaining almost nothing with

Him. At the time of His *Maha Samadhi,* only an amount of Rs. 16 in cash was found in His belongings as testified by Chakra Narayan who was Police fouzdar at Kopargaon and present there at Shirdi in October 1918 when Baba passed away:

> Whatever He got He scattered with a liberal hand. When He died, we took possession of His cash; that was only Rs. 16. Yet daily He was paying or giving away hundreds of rupees.

In the film *Shirdi Ke Sai Baba* there is a scene in which a *sadhu* comes from Haridwar to Shirdi and is amazed to see the grandeur of Shirdi Sai Baba's *palki* procession from Dwarka Mai to *Chavadi*, and wonders how a saintly person like Sai Baba prefers all this pomp and show; he takes Baba to be a hypocrite. But when he comes near Baba in Dwarka Mai Masjid and questions Baba about it, Baba shows him His miracle — giving the glimpse of the *sadhu's* Guru, which immediately brings him to the feet of Sai Baba.

In Sai literature, we find such references that in later years Baba used to receive plates full of delicious foods from His devotees, girls used to come and dance before Him in the *masjid*, people used to decorate Him with costly *chadars* (shawls) and clothes, He held His *durbar* like a majestic ruler. Yet, He was utterly indifferent to all this paraphernalia and accepted all this as an imposition of the wishes of His devotees on Him.

The following testimonies of Baba's contemporary devotees are most relevant in this respect:

i) Mrs. Manager testified as under:

> He (Baba) had no interests to serve or protect, no institution to seek support for or maintain: no acquisitions to safeguard; no private property to feel anxious about. Everything got was quickly disposed of. He lived on the begged and freely offered food.... When He died, He left in His pocket just the amount needed for His funeral expenses. His self-control and equanimity may be mentioned in this connection. He was far too lofty to care for trivial things. His palate, like His other senses, was so strictly under His control that none ever found Him to show any desire for anything, so far as I know.

ii) Das Ganu recalled:

> Several of those that he was regularly paying everyday were subjected to income tax. After Lokmanya Tilak visited Baba (1915-1917), the Income Tax Department directed its attention to the Shirdi *Samsthan*,

some officer came and watched the income. They first wanted to tax Sai Baba, but (perhaps seeing that He had little left with Him to proceed upon) they taxed His regular donors, viz., Tatya Patel, Bade Baba, Bagla and Bayaji Patel.

...He was really *advaita* personified. Thirty-two dancing girls would come and play before Him daily; He would never care to look at them. He never cared for anything. He was detached and in His *anand* state....

He used to cure the money-mindedness and the ego of His devotees by asking for *dakshina* repeatedly till they were left with no money. He advised none to become a *sanyasi* and forsake his family and home. He advised His devotees like Nana Saheb and Khaparde not to lust for sex. He advised Mlahaspati to sleep very little at night when he used to sleep with Baba in the Dwarka Mai Masjid.

In short, He Himself was following the kind of *yoga* which Guru Nanak spoke about while replying to *siddha* Lohadipa Yogi, and He advised His spiritually advanced devotees to follow the same scrupulously.

Where else except in the divine personality and role-functioning style of Shirdi Sai Baba do we find located in one personality the vibrant elements of Krishna's superb magnetism of love and knowledge of the reality of *atmagyan*, Buddha's aura of compassion and piety, Adi Shankara's *advaitism* and spirited fight against sectarianism and strict orthodoxy, Kabir's unconventional scathing attack on bigotry and obscuritism, Tulsi's devotion to Lord Rama and the devotional outpourings of love for the divine as those of the great integration like Mira, Chaitanya, Nanak, Purandhardasa, Thyagaraja, Kanakadasa, Tukaram, Ramadas, Narasimham, Mehta Ramanand, Nayanar Apar, Eknath, Namdev, Manikkavachakak, etc.; the mysticism of Rama Krishna Paramahansa and the love, brotherhood and service taught by Christ, Mohammed, Mother Teresa, Dalai Lama, Baba Amte and the like, and the philosophical musings of Ramana Maharshi, Sri Aurobindo and others? Sri Shirdi Sai Baba epitomised the quintessence of the values and ideals taught by the world's greatest religious and spiritual masters of all religions and lands in history.

People of all religions, nations and cultures have been and will always be finding all the previous values and spiritual truths in the life of Shirdi Sai Baba. Therefore, it is fully justified calling Shirdi Sai Baba the *Universal Master* of mankind — a unique *avatar* of God who descended in order to promote sublime form of spirituality and emotional integration among all human beings. The like of Him, who combined in His personality so diverse and ennobling attributes and lived such a simple life of *faqir*, has not yet been seen by the world, and who knows, the like of Him may not again be born at all! This makes Him a unique Universal Master of mankind whose most inspiring and spiritually elevating life story should be made known to people of all races, religions and lands.

One thing which is all the more unique about this great Universal Master is that although He shed His mortal coils in 1918, yet He even today responds to the earnest yearnings and prayers of all people in distress and of all His devotees as per unique assurances given by Him. We do not know of any other spiritual personality who had ever made such grand and compassionate assurances to mankind which still keep getting fulfilled. Evidently, a lot of research into the divine mysteries of Shirdi Sai Baba as the unique Universal Master of mankind is needed in order to understand Him. Baba's own advice in this connection was:

If a man utters My Name with love, I shall fulfil all his wishes, increase his devotion. If he earnestly listens to My life and deeds, him I shall beset in front and back and on all sides.

His Holiness Dalai Lama, the spiritual Head of the Tibetans, while delivering the Ninth Bhimsen Sachar Memorial lecture on 'Spiritual Values in Modern India', organised by the Servants of the People Society at Lajpat Bhawan, New Delhi, on 3 December, 1980, said:

The qualities of love and compassion are universal qualities which various religions try to develop among their adherents but religion is not a prerequisite which may be said to constitute a universal religion in themselves.... You don't need a complicated philosophy, you don't need a temple to develop these qualities.

Shirdi Sai Baba's total emphasis and compassion as has been shown above, was on such universal values of love, which are the basics of spirituality. He was not a promoter or champion of any religion as such; instead He was the teacher of spirituality which does not need a complicated philosophy, and that is why, Shirdi Sai Baba did not advance any complicated philosophy of His own, but emphasised the universal values and qualities. The religions may, in future, change or even disappear, as Rajneesh once prophesied, but the super spirituality of such simple universal values as preached and practised by Shirdi Sai Baba will ever remain alive and growing.

Neither rituals, O Lord Sai,
Nor the holy tulsi leaves,
Nor constant dips in the holy Ganges,
But true and loving devotion,
Only pleases and moves Thee
O Almighty, the Lord Sai.

—Sri Shirdi Sai Baba

12

Popularity

SRI Shirdi Sai Baba attained *Maha Samadhi* in 1918. During the last 76 years, His name and fame as a very great and highly benevolent and merciful saint, an incarnation of a very high stature, have spread throughout the nook and corner of the universe. In a miraculous manner, thousands of people of different religions and nationalities are becoming His devotees each day having come under the fold of His magnanimous grace and experiencing some sort of thrilling miracle in their lives. Temples devoted to Him have been coming up in different places, cities, towns and villages in India as well as in far off lands like USA, UK, African countries, Australia, Singapore, etc., due to the efforts of highly devoted self-motivated people. Innumerable devotees and rich donors vie with each other in providing funds and material for building and furnishing Shirdi Sai Temples that are coming up throughout the world as inspired by Him in many invisible and mysterious ways. Many charitable hospitals are run besides these temples and many welfare services and other charitable activities are being carried out by enthusiastic people in the name of Sri Shirdi Sai Baba. The number of devotees visiting Shirdi is ever increasing. In a nutshell, the devotional cult of Sri Shirdi Sai Baba is fast spreading throughout the world.

It is only because of Baba's mysterious divine wish and design that all these unique things are happening and Baba's eminence is fast spreading in concentric circles in all lands and all communities. Why is it that the appeal of Shirdi Sai Baba's charismatic personality is so irresistible to people? A. Sai devotee, B. Ramanatha Rao of Sai Kutir,

Popularity

Madras, has advanced the following reasons for it:

1. First and foremost because, in the words of Hemadpant, the author of *Shri Sai Sat Charita,* He (Shirdi Sai Baba) had taken a vow to give you what you want.

2. And that too immediately cash down; you ask with sincere devotion *(shraddha)* and patience *(saboori)* and there is the result.

3. He is so easily pleased. No hard penance, no unbearable fasts, not even difficult concentration and control of senses. In His words, "You look to Me and I will look to you." Can there be anything simpler than this?

4. He left His mortal body years ago and even today thousands of devotees have experienced His presence, having met their demands. What more guarantee is required?

5. Not being bodily present as a human being today, there is no danger of being cheated in His worship. In the case of so many *avatars, Bhagavans,* and *yogis* who have cropped up at present in the country, one is not sure if one is following the real preceptor *(sadguru).*

6. No money is required to worship Baba. He is pleased even with flowers, fruits, leaves or even water, devotionally offered. You do not even have to spend for travelling up to Shirdi. He is available even where you are, "even beyond the seven seas."

7. Ashes *(udi)* from the fire burning eternally in His Dwarka Mai is the cheapest and most infallible medicine for all diseases. The cost is only two paise — faith and patience.

8. His life history written by Hemadpant contains all the wisdom of the *Vedas,* the *Upanishads* and the *Gita* in the form of simple stories and anecdotes. Reading them alone and following the advice therein, one can reach the goal of liberation without fail.

9. Repetition of His name 'Sai' is so short, so sweet and so easy to pronounce; no twisting of tongue and difficult accents.

10. Last but not least, He on fulfilling your demands in this world, ensures that you do not get caught up in the dangerous web of this *sansar,* so He slowly moulds you, guides you and takes you step by step to liberation which is the key to enternal and everlasting bliss.

Shirdi Sai Baba's main insistence was on morality and simple and essential laws of spirituality which are universally emphasised by all religious scriptures, moral leaders and great personalities of all races and nations not on ritualistic religion as such. In matters of religion, He preached integration or unity of the genuine kind. He emphasised that all human beings and creatures have the same *atma* and, therefore, all are one and everyone in the living world is entitled to receive our love, hospitality, concern and help.

The world, as it is, is full of so many dissensions and social, cultural, economic and political conflicts, jealousies and immoral, disjunctive and disfunctional tendencies which have made the life of human beings all over the world very insecure. Religions have disappointed humanity through the doings of many fundamentalists, fanatics, hypocrites and wealth-loving and power-hankering Godmen, *yogis* and *acharyas* who rarely see eye to eye among themselves and do not feel shy in openly condemning each other. In such a social and religious context of the contemporary world, Shirdi Sai Baba alone comes up to the expectations of the masses of the world as the ideal Godman who epitomises simplicity, spirituality, love and genuine concern for all creatures, of the highest order. He combined in Him all the finest traits of the Vedic Gods, Adi Shankara, Christ, Buddha, Mahavir, Zoroaster, Mohammed, Nanak and all other great spiritual and religious personalities born in the world. Shirdi Sai Baba's charisma based on His simplicity, unconventionality, lack of diehard ritualiam, love and stress on unity and harmony is in utter contrast to the affluent and controversial lifestyles of many of the contemporary Godmen, *yogis* and *acharyas* captivates the hearts of people and is more than thereof anyone of the modern saints and Godmen. He is the most ideal saint who comes up to the expectations of most people of the world. The world is fed up with all those who teach religion, morality, spirituality and yoga and the like in enchanting words but crave for worldly properties, publicity, political patronage and all the pleasures and luxuries of modern life. Sri Shirdi Sai Baba, therefore, impresses us most.

It is also true that generally the modern educated people do not have much fascination for diehard ritualism. They do not have patience to do any kind of elaborate penance, *yagna, dhyana* or the like. They crave for simple, easy, readymade, instant benefits even in spiritual matters. They are cosmopolitan, secular and universal in their outlook and, therefore, do not wish to be confined to the narrow walls of their traditional religion and complicated incomprehensible rituals and customs. They crave for

Popularity 131

a broader, more sublime and easier-to-understand kind of spiritual experience. Shirdi Sai Baba's simple teachings are without any trappings of a complicated philosophy and His grace can be available to them just on remembering Him without any kind of difficulty or special effort. It is because of these reasons that Shirdi Sai Baba's name and fame have been spreading so fast throughout the world during the preceding seven decades and it continues spreading with ever growing tempo.

How Baba's Name is Spreading

Sri Shirdi Sai Sansthan, Shirdi, has been publishing valuable books and pictorial albums on Baba which have been spreading Baba's name and message throughout the world. Besides this, a number of organisations and voluntary bodies have come up to spread Baba's message. Sri Narasimha Swamiji established the All India Sai Samaj at Madras and authored a number of valuable books on Baba and spread His name and message throughout India. Sri Sai Sharananandji, Baba's noted contemporary devotee, authored a book *Sri Sai Baba* in Marathi and *Sri Sai The Superman* which have made Baba known throughout the world. Swami Karunananda and his son Shri Narayana Swami of Bhagawati Sai Sansthan, Panwel (Maharashtra) have been instrumental in spreading the teachings of Baba through their books, lectures and pioneering efforts to establish Sri Shirdi Sai Temples in UK, USA, Africa, Australia, etc. Sri Sai Samaj, Picket, Secunderabad (Andhra Pradesh), Sai Bhakhta Samaj, Delhi (Shirdi Sai Temple, 17, Institutional Area, Lodhi Road, New Delhi), Shirdi Sai Sabha, Chandigarh and other organisations have for years been doing remarkable service in the propagation of the message of Shirdi Sai Baba.

In Karnataka, a number of Shirdi Sai Temples have been established by the individual efforts of a highly devoted soul, Sri H. D. Laxman Swami. Sri Shivamma Thayee of Bangalore, a contemporary devotee of Shirdi Sai Baba, now 104 years of age, has inaugurated a number of Sri Shirdi Sai Temples and herself established three statues of Baba on His directions in her Sri Shirdi Sai Ashram, Roopen Agrahara, Maliwala, Bangalore.

In Rajasthan, a 74-years-old devotee, Kailash Bakiwala, has established a Shirdi Sai Temple at village Kukas, 17 kms from Jaipur on the Jaipur-Delhi road. In the author's recent meeting with him on 19 June, 1993, it was thrilling to learn from him that the place Kukas had been mentioned by the medieval poet Nabha Das of Galta (Jaipur) 400 years ago in his famous book *Bhakta Mal* in the following verse which states that a saint named Dwarka Das had established his *dhuni* at Kukas:

Sarita kookas gaon salil mein dhyan dhariyo man,
Ram charan anurag sudirad yanke sanchon man,
Soot kalatra dhan dhanya tahi soo sada udasi,
Kathin moh ko fand farki tori kul fansi,
Kilhe kripa bal bhajan ke gyan khang maya hani,
Ashtang yog tan tyagiyo Dwarika das jane dhuni.

It is the experience of not only Kailash Bakiwala, H. D. Laxman Swamiji and Shivamma Thayee but of almost all those who have been establishing Shirdi Sai Temples that Baba Himself has, through His mysterious ways, unknown persons and in strange circumstances, been ensuring that the construction and furnishing activities of the temples being newly constructed are carried out unexpectedly by the timely help in cash as well as kind at every step. Someone strangely appears to donate land, someone to donate the required bags of cement, someone comes up with the offer to provide fans, windows, etc., someone with funds to purchase marble and so on, without anyone asking for these things. These mysterious divine happenings are heard wherever one tries to discover how the new Sai Temples are coming up.

At many places, still more thrilling things (these are certainly miracles) have happened which have led to the establishment of Sri Shirdi Sai Temples on certain spots. Thus, for instance, several years back at Coimbatore a big cobra appeared and stayed there at a *Bhajan* session for several hours. People were convinced that it was nothing else but Sri Shirdi Sai Baba Himself and then a huge Nag Sai Temple was built on that very spot which has been attracting thousands of visitors every year. Similar miracles have indeed happened at many places in India and Sri Shirdi Sai Temples have sprung up and the name and fame of Baba and His universal message have thus been spreading all over. Instances like these compel even the extreme rationalists and iconoclasts among the modernites to believe in the mysterious supernatural powers and divine will of Shirdi Sai Baba which makes such things possible in the materialistic and selfish world of today.

There are many self-inspired and self-motivated devotees of Sri Shirdi Sai Baba belonging to Hindu, Jain, Christian, Parsi, Sikh and other religions who are on their own writing and publishing books on Baba, doing social service for the welfare of the poor and organising Sai *kirtans* and *bhajan* sessions for moral and spiritual uplift of mankind. Considerations of religion, race, caste, nationality, class, etc., do not come in the way of

Popularity

anyone becoming a Sai devotee and propagator of Baba's message. Thus, for instance, Zarine Taraporewalla, the English translator of Das Ganu's famous *Stavan Manjari* and K. J. Bhishma's *Sainath Sagunopasana* is a Parsee lady; Kailash Bakiwala of Jaipur, the founder of Sri Shirdi Sai Temple at Kukas (near Achrol, Jaipur district, Rajasthan) is a Jain; Bashir Baba, a great follower and propagator of Sri Shirdi Sai Baba (some believe that He Himself was Baba's incarnation) was a Muslim. There are many other such examples of devotees belonging to other religions, who are great devotees of Baba. There are also some foreign Christians of Austria, Australia and Canada who are great devotees of Shirdi Sai Baba. At Shirdi, one can see a middle-aged African lady attired in a white robe like a nun moving about *Gurusthan, Chavdi* and Dwarka Mai constantly or sitting with Sri Shivnesh Swamiji at *Gurusthan* and singing Kabir's songs at the *bhajan* sessions at *Chavadi*. All these concrete examples testify to the fact that the universal nature of Shirdi Sai Baba and the greatness and uniqueness of His divine message of brotherhood and love have indeed been understood by many enlightened people of different racial, national and religious backgrounds. Baba's 'Spiritual Socialism' has won the hearts of many people and the impact of His magnetism is thus going to attract more and more people's souls towards Him.

The very name of the Universal Master Sri Shirdi Sai unites the hearts and minds of people all over, releases the feeling of brotherhood, love and service among them and paves an easy and sure path to one's peaceful and contented life in the world and ultimate liberation.

In *Kaliyuga*, the name of Shirdi Sai Baba is thus a panacea for all the physical and spiritual ailments of mankind and more and more people are coming to realise this great fact and are therefore coming under the fold of His grace.

The role of Sri Sathya Sai Baba, the present incarnation of Shirdi Sai Baba, in spreading the name, fame, message and reverence of Shirdi Sai Baba, has been very significant. During the last 60 years, He has been revealing to the world the mysterious life, miracles and teachings of Shirdi Sai Baba and ceremonially doing *vibhuti abhishek* (washing with vibhuti) of Shirdi Sai Baba's silver statue in His Prasanthi Nilayam Ashram. All devotees of Sri Sathya Sai Baba, who number around three billion spread out in over 100 countries, invariably venerate and worship Shirdi Sai Baba and thus it can be said without any exaggeration that the name of Shirdi Sai Baba, the Universal Master, has already spread all over the whole globe. He is already in the hearts of many enlightened souls of over 100 countries. The time is fast coming when all the people of the world would hear His great name and become the followers of His message which teaches the very basics of morality and spirituality presented in only a few simple, direct and penetrating words full of love and wisdom.

It is firmly believed that it is only because of Shirdi Sai Baba's mysterious divine will that hitherto unknown facts about Baba's life are being disclosed and coming to light in mysterious ways. Thus for instance, Sri Sathya Sai Baba has disclosed the circumstances of Baba's birth, childhood and resurrection only during the last 2-3 years. Shivamma Thayee's memoirs highlighting Baba's miracles witnessed by her have been brought to the notice of the public in 1992. Only recently the facts of the rebirth of Mlahaspati as Sri Ranjit Kumar Trehan of Malyasia village in Punjab, the rebirth of Abdul as Ken, a Canadian of Japanese birth, the rebirth of Chand Bhai Patil as a Muslim in Maharashtra have come to light. It is only because of Baba's wish that Mlahaspati's lifesize statue has been established in Khandoba Temple at Shirdi by Sri Ranjit Kumar Trehan.

It has been discovered by us in the course of our research on Baba that He was gracious enough to manipulate circumstances in such a manner that His close and ardent devotees like Mlahaspati and H. S. Dixit, passed away on the auspicious day of *Ekadasi*. Mlahaspati died on 11 September 1922 on *Ekadasi Somvar* in the month of Bhadrapada; Kaka H. S. Dixit also died on *Ekadasi* on 5 July, 1926. Baba's other devotees like Abdul, Hemadpant, Das Ganu and others also had a peaceful end. Baba Himself appeared in the dreams of H.S. Dixit and Dabholkar the night before their deaths. This shows that Baba sees to it that His ardent devotees leave this world on an auspicious *tithi* (day) so that they achieve liberation. This research-finding has a great lesson for all of us.

Recently, on 19 June, 1993, the author went to Jaipur on some personal work. By Sai Baba's mysterious divine plan, he was introduced to Sri Kailash Bakiwala (26A, Chetak Marg, near Jaykeylon Mother-Child Hospital, Moti Doongri Road, Jaipur). In the course of talks, He revealed to the author that He had in his possession a photostat copy of a letter from Shirdi Sai Baba written by Shama in Hindi, to the then Thakur, *Jagirdar* of Achrol Thikana (approximately 20 kms from Jaipur), about 134 years back. The original letter is stated to be with Sri Kailash Bakiwala's wife's sister's son Shravan Kumar, an antique dealer who lives near Mahavir Park, Kishanpole Bazar, Jaipur city. This letter was

Popularity

in response to one written by Thakur Hari Singhji of Achrol, father of the present *Jagirdar* of Achrol to Sri Shirdi Sai Baba who, he had met at Mount Abu hill station. Author E. Bhardwaja in his book *Sai Baba The Master* quoting Dr. K. S. Gawankar's book on Sai Baba has referred to Sai Baba's following statement to His devotees, Bade Baba and Bapugir Gosavi:

> I grew up in Mahurgad; when people pestered me I left for Girnar, there too people troubled Me much and I left for Mount Abu. There too the same thing happened. Then I came to Akkalkote and from there to Daulatabad. There Janardhana Swami did me a lot of seva. Then I went to Pandarpur, from there I came to Shirdi.

This reveals that Shirdi Sai had visited Mount Abu sometime during the summer of 1858 and Thakur Hari Singh of Achrol (Jaipur) during His summer stay at that hill station met the young Sai who was then about 20 years of age. With this acquaintance, Thakur Hari Singh wrote a letter to Sai Baba in response to which Sai Baba got the following letter written by His close devotee Shama, schoolmaster, and sent to Thakur Hari Singh. The letter is a bit torn and some words of it are thus missing. The rest of the letter is as under:

SRI RAMJI (ALLAH)

Sidh Shri....Sri Thakur Ke...Joglikhant Daulat...Sai Saheb Selani aa pahunche. hum khushi hain...ki khushi chahte hain aap ko Allah khush rakhe aur...ji main hum roj lot pot ho jate hain. Khush raho abad raho Faqir ki yahi dua hai aur sab se dua kahna raji rahna.

The English rendering of this letter, the only letter of Sai Baba so far discoverd, is as under:

SRI RAMJI (ALLAH)

To Sri Thakur...this letter is being written to you...Sai Sahib the wanderer has reached here, we are well...we wish you well and may Allah keep you happy. We are in bliss daily. Be happy, be prosperous, this is the blessing of Baba faqir and convey our blessing to all and be happy.

The letter could be of any date between 1858 and 1890, most probably of 1858, soon after Baba's arrival at Shirdi. It is likely that Baba might have told Raja Hari Singh that He would be reaching and permanently staying at Shirdi after leaving Mount Abu and he could write to Him there.

Kailash Bakiwala informed the author that the original letter of Shirdi Sai Baba was discovered by a *kabadi* (waste articles dealer) from the old books and papers sold by the family of Achrol Thakur about 5 years back; the *kabadi* discovered this letter and finding it to be of some importance gave it to a painter of Jaipur; the painter's income from his paintings suddenly increased from the day this auspicious letter came into his custody. This letter then somehow passed into the hands of Sravan Kumar of Jaipur and from him Kailash Bakiwala could manage to get its photostat copy.

The fact that the discovery of Shirdi Sai Baba's only letter came to be known to the author, when he was to write the last chapter of this book in the second fortnight of June 1993, most unexpectedly and mysteriously without any effort is by itself an evidence of Sri Shirdi Sai Baba's divine *leela* which makes such miracles happen. It shows that the Divine Master wished that His letter should now, after about a century, be made known to the world at large through this book.

Baba's mysteries, miracles and graces are really mind-boggling, endless, too diverse and too deep to understand. The most that one can and should do in this life is to keep on singing His most holy Name *'SRI SAI'* from the core of one's heart, placing all things, all worries, hopes and aspirations at His lotus Feet, believing firmly in Baba's assurance "Why Fear, When I Am Here".

APPENDIX - I

Pilgrimage to Shirdi

SHIRDI Sai Baba's place, Shirdi (Maharashtra state) is a very sacred, powerful and important place of pilgrimage in India. One can visit this holy place easily. It is a well developed town connected by bus routes. There is an important Railway Station Manmad through which the Karnataka Express from New Delhi to Bangalore passes. A number of trains from Bombay and Delhi also pass through this station. Shirdi is only about 58 kms. from Manmad and buses and taxis are easily available to reach there. The distance of Shirdi from some important cities is as under:

Bombay	-	266 kms.	Nasik	-	122 kms.
Hyderabad	-	610 kms.	Surat	-	373 kms.
Nagpur	-	618 kms.	Jalgaon	-	233 kms.
Ahmednagar	-	83 kms.	Delhi	-	1166 kms.
Pune	-	207 kms.	Sholapur	-	312 kms.

There are arrangements for lodging and boarding at Shirdi Sai Sansthan but since the crowd of people on all days, especially on Thursdays is very large, many are unable to get accommodation, they have to seek the same in hotels, lodging places and private houses. Although there are arrangements for selling breakfast, lunch and dinner packets at the *Sansthan,* yet due to heavy rush most people have to eat outside in the market.

Routine at Shirdi
The *Kakad arti* is performed in the early morning at 5.15 a.m. when Lord Sri Sai Baba is awakened from His sleep. Then the *Samadhi* and idol are washed ceremonially and clad, everyday from 6 a.m. to 7 a.m. Records of Sai Geet and Mangal Shehnai are played at both times. Then individual *abhisheks* are started at 7.30 a.m. The collective *abhishek* starts at 11 a.m.

The noon *arti* takes place exactly at noon. Nobody is allowed to go up to the idol over the *Samadhi* after this *arti*. Then there is a programme of singing, *bhajan* and *kirtan* in the afternoon. There is again *arti* at 6.30 p.m. (sunset time). Then there is *kirtan* or *bhajan* till 10 p.m. and the last *arti*, i.e., *Shej-arti* takes place at 10 p.m. A mosquito net is covered over the idol and the Samadhi and Lord Sri Sai Baba are thereafter deemed to have gone to sleep.

On Thursdays, there is a procession of the *palki* and the *padukas* at night and five gunshots are fired at the time of the procession. Loudspeakers are arranged at the time of *arti* and the festival day's programmes.

Important Places at Shirdi
A visitor to Shirdi should invariably visit the following places:

1. *Samadhi Mandir*

The construction of the Samadhi Mandir was started by Sri Buti during the lifetime of Sai Baba, with a view to having a temple of Sri Murlidhar. At a time when the construction was almost complete, Sai Baba said that he could stay over there. So after Sai Baba attained *Nirvana,* His mortal remains were buried at the place. The white marble pavement of the *Samadhi* was made afterwards. The marble statue prepared by sculptor Sri Talim was installed by the side of the *Samadhi* in 1954. The spacious hall in front of the *Samadhi* was also paved with marble tiles later. The people, coming for *darshan,* come first in the hall, which is decorated with photos of the saints and devotees of Sai Baba. The statue of Sai Baba, in a sitting position is such that He looks to every devotee coming for *darshan* in the hall. In a room, on the left side of the hall, the articles used by Sai Baba are exhibited. There is a cellar below the right-side rooms where valuables are kept. There is a gallery on the first floor and several rooms which can be used by the devotees.

2. *Dwarka Mai Masjid*

This was an old *Masjid* named as Dwarka Mai by Sai Baba Himself. He lived here all day and used to sit on a big stone, which is still preserved. A portrait of Sai Baba, painted during His lifetime, is also kept here. In front of the portrait, the sacred *dhuni* (fire) kindled by Sai Baba is kept burning since then. A grinding stone, a bathing stone, a wooden pillar, *chulha, padukas* and Tulsi Vrindavan, which were used by Sai Baba are all maintained here. *Rath* and pallanquin are also kept here in a small room. The *udi,* taken out from the ever-blazing *dhuni,* is used by the devotees as miraculous ash.

Appendices

3. *Chavadi*
It is to the east of Dwarka Mai. Sai Baba used to rest at this place every alternate night. A number of portraits of deities are exhibited here since the days of Sai Baba. A wooden plank and a wheeled chair used by Sai Baba, are also kept here.

4. *Gurusthan*
This is the place of Sai Baba's Guru. Sai Baba used to sit here under a *neem* tree, leaves of which lost their bitterness due to the grace of Sai Baba. Incense is burnt here day and night in a pot, in front of the *mandir*, wherein Lord Shiva's *pindi* and Nandi are installed and *padukas* of Lord Sai Baba are also kept.

5. *Lendibag and Nandadeep*
Lendi *nalla* was flowing through this land and there was a burial ground at the place. Sai Baba dug a well here and He used to take out drinking water from it. Now the Lendi *nalla* is filled and a garden is laid there. A *Nandadeep* is kept burning there since the day of Sai Baba, Who used to sit here on a *par* (stone otla) near the Nandadeep below the *neem* tree. This *park* is rennovated and maintained. A new Datta *mandir* has been built in the garden in front of the *ashwattha* tree. There is the *Samadhi* of the horse Shamsunder, who used to bow down to Sai Baba and thereafter to the *Samadhi* daily till its death. There are the *Samadhis* of Baba's devotees Abdul Baba, Nanavalli, Bhau Maharaj and Tatya at the entrance of the Lendibag.

6. *Khandoba Mandir*
This is a small temple situated on Ahmednagar-Kopargaon road. It was at this temple that Sai Baba was first greeted by Sri Mlahaspati as *"Ya, Sai"*

7. *Mahadev, Shani and Ganesh temples*
These three temples are built in a line. The Mahadev *mandir* is very old and a statue of a tiger has been installed behind the Nandi. There is a *dhuni* in the Shani *mandir* also. The Ganesh Temple is also very old. There are Keshav *mandir* and *Mangal Karyalaya*, built in recent years beyond the road on the eastern side.

APPENDIX - II

Baba's Worship :
108 Names of Sai Baba

1. Om Shree Sainathaya Namah
2. Om Lakshmi Narayanaya Namah
3. Om Krishna-Rama-Shiv-Marutyadi Roopaya Namah
4. Om Sheshashayene Namah
5. Om Godavari Tata Sheeladheewasine Namah
6. Om Bhaktahridalayaya Namah
7. Om Sarvahrinnilayaya Namah
8. Om Bhootawasaya Namah
9. Om Bhoota-Bhawishyat Bhawawarjitaya Namah
10. Om Kalateetaya Namah
11. Om Kalaya Namah
12. Om Kalakalaya Namah
13. Om Kaladarpadamanaya Namah
14. Om Mrutunjayaya Namah
15. Om Amartyaya Namah
16. Om Martyamayapradaya Namah
17. Om Jeewadharaya Namah
18. Om Sarwadharaya Namah
19. Om Bhaktawanasamarthaya Namah
20. Om Bhaktawanapratidnayaya Namah
21. Om Anna Vastradaya Namah

22. Om Aarogyakshemadaya Namah
23. Om Dhanamangalyapradaya Namah
24. Om Riddhisiddhidaya Namah
25. Om Putra-Mitra-Kalatra-Bandhudaya Namah
26. Om Yogakshemawahaya Namah
27. Om Aapbandhawaya Namah
28. Om Margabandhawaya Namah
29. Om Bhuktimuktishwargaprawargadaya Namah
30. Om Priyay Namah
31. Om Preetiwardhanaya Namah
32. Om Antaryamine Namah
33. Om Satchidatmane Namah
34. Om Nityanandaya Namah
35. Om Paramsukhadaya Namah
36. Om Parameshwaraya Namah
37. Om Para Brahmane Namah
38. Om Paramatmane Namah
39. Om Dhyanaswaroopine Namah
40. Om Jagatah-pitre Namah
41. Om Bhaktanam-matri-dhatri-pitamahaya Namah
42. Om Bhaktabhayapradaya Namah
43. Om Bhaktaparadheenaya Namah
44. Om Bhaktanugrahakatarya Namah
45. Om Sharnagatawatsalaya Namah
46. Om Bhaktishaktipradaya Namah
47. Om Gyan Vairagyapradeya Namah
48. Om Prempradaya Namah
49. Om Sanshaya-Hridayadurbalya-Papakarma Wasana Kshayakaraya Namah
50. Om Hridaya Granthi Bhedkaya Namah
51. Om Karmadhwansine Namah
52. Om Shuddasatwasthitaya Namah

53. Om Gunateetagunatmane Namah
54. Om Anantakalyangunaya Namah
55. Om Amitaparakramaya Namah
56. Om Jayine Namah
57. Om Durdharshaakshobhyaya Namah
58. Om Aparajitya Namah
59. Om Trilokeshu-Awiqhatqataye Namah
60. Om Sarwashaktimoortaye Namah
61. Om Akshakyarahitaya Namah
62. Om Swaroop Sundaraya Namah
63. Om Sulochanaya Namah
64. Om Bahuroowishwamoortaye Namah
65. Om Aroopaawyaktaya Namah
66. Om Achintyaya Namah
67. Om Sookshmaya Namah
68. Om Sarwantaryamine Namah
69. Om Manowagateetaya Namah
70. Om Prem-moortaye Namah
71. Om Sulabhadurlabhaya Namah
72. Om Asahayasahayaya Namah
73. Om Anathanathadeenbandhawe Namah
74. Om Sarwabharbhrite Namah
75. Om Akarmanekakarmasukarmine Namah
76. Om Punnyasharawankeertanaya Namah
77. Om Teerthaya Namah
78. Om Vasudevaya Namah
79. Om Satam-Gataye Namah
80. Om Satparayanya Namah
81. Om Lokanathaya Namah
82. Om Pawananaghaya Namah
83. Om Amritnashawe Namah

84. Om Bhaskerprabhaya Namah
85. Om Brahmacharya-Tapashcharyadisuswrataya-Namah
86. Om Satyadharmaparayanaya Namah
87. Om Siddheshwaraya Namah
88. Om Siddhasankalpaya Namah
89. Om Yogeshwaraya Namah
90. Om Bhagawate Namah
91. Om Bhaktawatsalaya Namah
92. Om Satpurushaya Namah
93. Om Pusushottamaya Namah
94. Om Satyatatwabodhakya Namah
95. Om Kamadishadwairidhwansine Namah
96. Om Abhedanandanubhawapradaya Namah
97. Om Samasarwamatsammataya Namah
98. Om Shree Dakshinamoortye Namah
99. Om Shree Venkateshramanaya Namah
100. Om Adbhutanandacharyaya Namah
101. Om Prapannartiharaya Namah
102. Om Sansarasarwadukhakshayakaraya Namah
103. Om Sarwawitsaktomukhaya Namah
104. Om Sarwantarbhisthitaya Namah
105. Om Sarwamangalakaraya Namah
106. Om Sarwabheeshtapradaya Namah
107. Om Samarasasanmargastha-Panaya Namah
108. Om Shree Samarthasadguru Sainathaya Namah.

A Select Bibliography

1. Agaskar, P.S., *Sri Sai Leelamrita*. Shirdi: Sri Sai Baba Sansthan, 1989 (In Hindi), pp. 202.
2. Aiyer, P.S.V., *Perfect Masters*. Calcutta: Author, 1973, pp. 58.
3. Bhardwaja, E., *Sai Baba: The Master*. Ongole: Sri Guru Paduka Publications, 1991 (III Ed.), pp. 392.
4. "Sai Baba: God's Precious Gift to India," *Blitz*, (Bombay), September 29, 1979.
5. Bhisma, K.J., *Sri Sadguru Sai Nath - Sagunopasana*. Sri Shirdi Sai Baba Sansthan, 1986 (In Marathi), pp. 36.
6. Ganu, Das, *Shri Sainath: Stavan Manjari*. Shirdi: Sri Sai Baba Sansthan (English translation by Zarina Taraporwala).
7. *Gems of Wisdom*. Nagpur: Sri Publications. pp. 19.
8. Gunaji, N.V., *Shri Sai Satcharita* (The Wonderful Life and Teachings of Shri Sai Baba); Shirdi: Shirdi Sansthan, 1982 (X Ed.), pp. 274.
9. *Guide to Holy Shirdi*. Shirdi: Shri Sai Baba Sansthan, pp. 20.
10. Juneja, B. *Shirdi Ke Sai Baba Aur Unka Jeevan*. Delhi: Pooja Prakashan, Qutab Road, Sadar, May, 1991, pp. 64 (In Hindi).
11. Junnarkar, R.S., *A Mission Divine*. Bombay: Prasanthi Prakashan, 1890, pp. 511.
12. Kamath, M.V. & Kher, V.B., *Sai Baba of Shirdi: A Unique Saint*, Bombay: Jaico Publishing House, 1991, pp. 316.
13. Karunanand, Swami, *The Uniqueness of the Significance of Sri Sai Baba*. Bombay: Sri Bhagawati Sai Sansthan.

A Select Bibliography 145

14. Kharparde, G. *Sources of Sai History*, Bangalore: The Jupiter Press (Diary 1910, 1911, 1912).
15. -------------- , *Shirdi Diary*. Bombay: Sri Sai Baba Sansthan, pp. 141 (Events between December 1910 and March 1918).
16. Krishna, Indira Anantha, *Sai Baba of Shirdi*. Adarsh Chitra Katha (Pictorial), pp. 32.
17. Kumar, Anil, *Doctor of Doctors Sri Sai Baba*. Nagpur, Sri Sai Clinic, Chitar - Oal, pp. 9.
18. Kumar, Sudhir, *Shirdi Ke Sai Baba; Chalisa Aur Bhajan*. New Delhi: Author, pp. 64. (In Hindi)
19. Mehta, Rao Saheb Harshad B, *The Spiritual Symphony of Shree Sainath of Shirdi*. Baroda; Rana & Patel Indira Press, 1952.
20. Menen, Aubrey, *The New Mystics and the True Indian Tradition*. London; Thames & Hudson, 1974, pp. 192.
21. Murthy, T.S.A, *Life and Teachings of Sri Sai Baba of Shirdi*. Bangalore: 140, 4th Main Road, Malleswaram, 1974, pp. 177.
22. Narasimhamswamiji; *Who is Sri Sai Baba of Shirdi?* Madras: All India Sai Samaj, pp. 23.
23. -------------- , *Sri Sai Vachnamrita*. Madras, 1968 (In Hindi).
24. -------------- , The *Wondrous Saint Sai Baba*. Madras. All India Sai Samaj pp. 110.
25. -------------- , *Life of Sai Baba*. Madras: All India Sai Samaj, Vol. II, pp. 402, Vol. IV, pp. 240, 1956.
26. -------------- , *Devotees' Experiences of Sri Sai Baba*. Hyderabad: Akhanda Sainama Saptha Samithi, 1989 (Vol. I, II, III).
27. Osbourne Arthur, *The Incredible Sai*. New Delhi: Orient Longman Ltd.
28. Pradhan, Moreshwar W., *Sri Sai Baba of Shirdi* (I Ed., 1933) Shirdi: Shirdi Sansthan, 1973 (VII Ed), pp. 63.
29. Parchure, S.D., *Shree Sai Mahimahastra*. Bombay : Taradeo Book Depot 1990, pp. 22.
30. *Pictorial Sai Baba*. Shirdi: Sri Sai Baba Sansthan, 1968.
31. Parchure, D.L, *Children's Sai Baba*. Shirdi: Shirdi Sansthan, 1991, pp. 46.

32. Puri. J.K., *Thus Spake Shirdi Sai Baba.* Chandigarh. Shirdi Sai Sabha.
33. Ramalingaswamy, *Golden Words Of Sri Sai Baba of Shirdi.* Shirdi: Munja Baba Sasthan, 1985, pp. 66.
34. Rao, K.V. Raghav, *Messages of Sri Sai Baba.* Madras: All India Sai Samaj, 1984 pp. 28.
35. Rigopolous, Antonio, *The Life and Teachings of Sri Sai Baba of Shirdi.* Delhi : Sri SadGuru Publications, Indian Books Centre (40/5, Shakti Nagar, Delhi - 110 007), 1993. (First published by New State University Press of New York in 1992). This is the only Ph. D. work published on Sri Shirdi Sai Baba in the world (Ph. D. Degree awarded by the University of Venice, Italy in 1987.)
36. Ruhela, S.P., *Sri Shirdi Sai Baba Avatar — A Comprehensive and Uptodate Research based Profile.* Faridabad : Sai Age Publications (126, Sector 37), 1992.
37. ------------ , *My Life with Sri Shirdi Sai Baba — Thrilling Memoirs of Shivamma Thayee, 102 years Old Lady, the Only Surviving Direct Devotee of Sri Shirdi Sai Baba.* Faridabad : Sai Age Publications (126, Sector 37), 1992.
38. ------------ , *What Researchers Say on Sri Shirdi Sai Baba.* Faridabad : Sai Age Publications (126, Sector 37), 1994.
39. ------------ , *The Sai Trinity.* New Delhi, Vikas Publishing House (576, Masjid Road, Jungpura, New Delhi - 110 014), 1994.
40. Sahukar, Mani, *Sai Baba : The Saint of Shirdi.* Bombay: Somaiya Publications.
41. *Sai Sandesh.* Hyderabad : Sai Prabha Publications, (3-5-697-A, Telugu Academy lane, Vinalwadi, Narayangulu), 1990.
42. Sai Sharananand, *Sri Sai Baba* (In Marathi). Bombay: Dinpushpa Prakashan, 1982 pp. 474.
43. *Sri Sai The Superman.* Shirdi: Shri Shirdi Sansthan, 1991, pp. 139.
44. *Sanathana Sarathi,* November, 1990; November 1992.
45. *Saptahik Hindustan* (Hindi Weekly), Nov. 22, 1992. (Special issue on Shirdi Sai Baba).
46. Sholapurkar, G.R., *Foot-Prints at Shirdi and Puttaparthi.* Delhi: Bharatiya Vidya Prakashan, 1989 (II Ed).

A Select Bibliography

47. *Shirdi Darshan*. Shirdi: Sri Sai Baba Sansthan, 1972, 1966 (Pictorial).
48. *Shirdi Ke Sai Baba*. Delhi: Ratan Book Co. (242, Gali Kunjas, Dariba Kalan) (In Hindi).
49. Shivnesh Swamiji. *Sri Sai Bavani*. Shirdi, pp. 11 (In Hindi).
50. *Shree Sai Leela : Sachitra Jivandarshan*, 1939 (Pictorial) pp. 34.
51. *Shree Sai Leela :* March-April 1992 Issue (First Convention of Sai Devotees), pp. 66.
52. *Sri Sai Chalisa*. Nagpur: Sai Publications (In Hindi).
53. *Sri Sai Gita*. Nagpur: Sai Publications (In Hindi).
54. *Souvenir :* Maha Samadhi Souvenir. Madras: All India Sai Samaj 1966.
55. *Souvenir :* Delhi: Shri Sai Bhakth Samaj, 1972.
56. *Souvenir :* Secunderabad: Sri Sai Baba Samajam, 1975.
57. *Souvenir :* Secunderabad: Sri Sai Baba Samajam, 1990, pp. 160.
58. *Souvenir:* 26 All India Sai Devotees' Convention: Golden Jubilee Year 1991.
59. *Souvenir :* Faridabad: Shirdi Sai Baba Temple Society, Sai Dham, Tigaon Road, 1994.
60. *Tales of Sai Baba*. Bombay: India Book House (Pictorial).
61. Tanavde, S.V, *May Sai Baba Bless Us All*. Bombay: Taradeo Book Depot pp. 48.
62. Taraporwala, Zarine; *Worship of Manifested Sri Sadguru Sainath*. (English Translation of K.J. Bhishma's *Sri Sadguru Sainath Sagunopāsna*) Bombay: Saidhun Enterprises, 1990, pp. 39.
63. *Your Questions and Sri Sai Baba's Answers*. Bombay: Madhav B.K. Lele, pp. 72 (In Hindi).
64. White Charles, S.J, "The Sai Baba Movement; Approaches to the Study of Indian Saint," *The Journal of Asian Studies* (Vol, XXXI, No.4) August 1972. Also reprinted in : Ruhela, S.P. (Ed.) *Sai Baba Movement*. New Delhi: Arnold Heineman Publishers, 1985.

JOURNALS

Shri Sai Leela (Bi-monthly): Official Organ of Shirdi Sai Sansthan, Sai Niketan 804-B, Dr. Ambedkar Road, Dadar, Bombay-400 014. (Annual Subscription Rs. 50/-).

Sai Sudha: All India Samaj, Mylapore, Madras.

Sai Kripa: (Official Organ of Sai Bhakta Samaj, Delhi), Shirdi Sai Temple, 17, Institutional Area, Lodhi Road, New Delhi-110 003. (Quarterly).

As far as known to us, the following organisations are doing excellent work in spreading the message of Sri Shirdi Sai Baba:

1. Shirdi Sai Sansthan, Shirdi (Maharashtra).
2. All India Sai Samaj, Mylapore, Madras.
3. Sri Sai Samaj, Picket, Secunderabad.
4. Shirdi Sai Sabha, Chandigarh.
5. Sri Bhagawati Sai Sansthan, Panvel (Maharashtra).
6. Sai Publications, Red Cross Road, Civil Lines, Nagpur.